AMERICAN AUTHORS
AND CRITICS SERIES

GENERAL EDITOR

JOHN MAHONEY

University of Detroit

F. SCOTT FITZGERALD (about 1925)

F. SCOTT FITZGERALD

An Introduction and Interpretation

MILTON HINDUS

Brandeis University

Hard-bound edition distributed by
BARNES & NOBLE, INC.
Publishers · Booksellers · New York

Grateful acknowledgment is made to Charles Scribner's Sons for their generosity in permitting the author to quote from the various novels and stories by F. Scott Fitzgerald. Among them are: *This Side of Paradise,* copyright 1920; *The Beautiful and Damned,* copyright 1922; *The Great Gatsby,* copyright 1925; "The Rich Boy," copyright 1926; *Tender Is the Night,* copyright 1934; *The Last Tycoon,* copyright 1945.

Quotations from the works of F. Scott Fitzgerald are fully protected by copyright and are reprinted by special permission of Charles Scribner's Sons.

Quotations on pages 52, 55, 60, and 61 from the Introduction by Malcolm Cowley to the revised edition of *Tender Is the Night* by F. Scott Fitzgerald, pages x, xv, xxi, are also used by permission of Charles Scribner's Sons.

In addition, acknowledgment is made to:
The Bodley Head Scott Fitzgerald Vol. III for quotes from *The Crack-Up.*

New Directions for one line from Ezra Pound's "Hugh Selwyn Mauberly" in *The Crack-Up.* "From Ezra Pound, *Personae.* Copyright 1926, 1953 by Ezra Pound. Reprinted by permission of New Directions Publishing Corporation."

New Directions for selections from *The Crack-Up.* Copyright 1934, 1936 by Esquire, Inc., 1945 by New Directions. Reprinted by permission of New Directions Publishing Corporation.

Random House, Inc., for "In Memory of W. B. Yeats" by W. H. Auden. From *The Collected Poems of W. H. Auden,* © 1960.

Harold Ober Associates, Inc., for quotes from *The Moral of F. Scott Fitzgerald* by Glenway Wescott.

Houghton Mifflin Company for quotes from *The Far Side of Paradise* by Arthur Mizener. Copyright 1951.

Harcourt, Brace & World, Inc., for lines from "The Hollow Men" and "The Waste Land" from *Collected Poems 1909–1962* by T. S. Eliot.

The Dial Press for quotes from *Men Seen* by Paul Rosenfeld.

Edmund Wilson and John Dos Passos for their contributions in *The Crack-Up*.

Andrew Turnbull for quotes from his *Scott Fitzgerald*.

ABOUT THE AUTHOR

WHEN Brandeis University was founded in Massachusetts in 1948, Milton Hindus became one of the thirteen members of the original faculty. A professor of English, he held the Peter and Elizabeth Walkenstein chair at the University from 1965 to 1967. He has taught at The University of Chicago, The University of California at Los Angeles, New York University, Hunter College, The New School, and The College of the City of New York. He is the author of *The Crippled Giant, The Proustian Vision,* and *A Reader's Guide to Marcel Proust.* The Walt Whitman Prize was awarded to Professor Hindus by The Poetry Society of America for his *Leaves of Grass: One Hundred Years After.* His essays and book reviews have appeared in numerous publications including *The New York Times Book Review, The Chicago Tribune Speaking of Books, The New Leader, Atlantic Monthly, Sewanee Review, Kenyon Review, The New Republic, Poetry Magazine, The Virginia Quarterly Review, Commentary,* and *The Southern Review.*

To Eva

PREFACE

THE WRITER of this book may share the feeling with his reader that too much has already been written about F. Scott Fitzgerald. It is a law of publicity that those who need it least receive it most. The law holds true for literary men as well: those who already have a great deal seem effortlessly to pick up more and more.

But it is fortunate when lasting quality—as in Fitzgerald's case—rather than merely ephemeral fashion, exacts such a tribute. Yet the cairns of criticism which mark the places even of the classics present a problem to the reader with limited time at his disposal. How is he to distinguish the contributions of personal piety from those of more impersonal insight? Even in the best critical essays the motivations are sometimes mixed, and the reader who passes them by to grapple with a masterwork directly is not to be blamed but commended for his initiative. In fact, the best commentary is meant to be read after we have fed our curiosity upon the original text rather than before.

Although I have learned much from other criticisms of Fitzgerald, I have rarely if ever been completely satisfied with them. It seemed to me that critics conceived of their role usually as that of defense attorneys for their subject, or, more rarely, as that of district attorneys bringing an indictment against him. Such one-sided attitudes cloud the judgment and are less than helpful in achieving an objective evaluation of an author.

In retrospect, the "problem" in Fitzgerald which intrigues me perhaps more than any other is the distinction which his career invites us to make between art and life. In few other contemporary creators are we conscious of such a sensational gap between "the man that suffers and the mind that creates." Or, as Proust states in his *Contre Sainte-Beuve*: "a book is the product of a different *self* from the self we manifest in our habits, in our social life, in our vices." Like some other accursed poets from Villon to Rimbaud, Fitzgerald compensated for the almost contemptible shortcomings of his conduct with an art which brought new life to the English language. At its best, it is not unworthy of Fitzgerald's own description of Keats's work: his greatest things (almost all of them composed in the years from 1924 to 1926) supply "a scale of workmanship for anybody who wants to know truly about words, their most utter value for evocation, persuasion or charm. . . . Granted an ear, one could scarcely ever afterwards be unable to distinguish between gold and dross in what one read."

I have in the text tried to appraise Fitzgerald's accomplishment as it might appear through the eyes of one who has pondered the meaning of the critical standards suggested by a man like the late Irving Babbitt. I have attempted to measure his performance more or less precisely and without falling into the errors of excess or niggardliness which have characterized some of the past critical studies of him. I regard him as being part of the second wave or backwash of that romantic movement, the first wave of which crested in the early decades of the nineteenth century. Essentially he has repeated, though with some variations, both the errors and triumphs of his predecessors, whom he never ceased reading about and with whom, we know, he justifiably felt a great affinity.

I should like, at this point, to thank Professor John Mahoney and Mr. Andrew Turnbull for reading my manuscript, or large portions of it, and for commenting upon what they have read. I wish also to recall here the enthusiastic insight into the works of Fitzgerald which I found in my talks with David Ignatow and Maurice Hindus, whose inspiration helped in making this study.

M. H.

Newton Centre, Mass.
December 1967

viii

CONTENTS

CHRONOLOGY

1894   Francis Scott Fitzgerald born September 24. Only child of Edward Fitzgerald and Mary (McQuillan) Fitzgerald.

1898   Family moved to Buffalo, New York, by firm of Procter and Gamble, employers of Mr. Fitzgerald.

1901   Moved to Syracuse for same reason.

1903   Moved back to Buffalo. Primary education at the Holy Angels Convent.

1908   Mr. Fitzgerald fired from job in March. Family back in St. Paul by July. Lived mostly on Grandfather McQuillan's money on the periphery of St. Paul's finest residential district "in the neighborhood of Summit Avenue." Scott sent to St. Paul Academy.

1911   Sent to Newman Academy in Boston. Met Father Fay to whom *This Side of Paradise* is dedicated.

1913   Went to Princeton University. Met Edmund Wilson and John Peale Bishop as fellow students and Christian Gauss as teacher. Poor freshman year academically because of extracurricular activities preparing Triangle Club show.

1915   Withdrew from Princeton in November due to serious physical illness as well as unsatisfactory academic record.

1916   Returned to Princeton in September stubbornly determined to start over again but still judged academically ineligible. Deluged undergraduate literary magazine with contributions of nine poems, five book reviews, and eight stories.

1917   Received army commission as Second Lieutenant in October. Did not get overseas.

1918   Met Zelda Sayre in July.

1919   Discharged from the army. Took job with advertising agency.

1920   *This Side of Paradise* published by Scribner's in March. Was a popular success. Married Zelda Sayre, April 3. Collection of stories, *Flappers and Philosophers,* published in August.

1921   Daughter, Frances Scott Fitzgerald, born. She was to be an only child, like himself.

1922 Novel *The Beautiful and Damned* published. Second collection of short stories, *Tales of the Jazz Age,* published.

1923 Play *The Vegetable,* upon which great financial hopes were staked, a failure.

1924 Trip to the Riviera in the summer. Winter in Rome.

1925 *The Great Gatsby,* successful both as a novel and in its adaptation as a play, published. Fitzgeralds in Paris in the spring.

1926 Collection of short stories, *All the Sad Young Men,* published. Included one of his finest efforts, "The Rich Boy."

1927 First trip to Hollywood.

1928 In Paris for the summer.

1929 Moved abroad.

1930 Zelda's mental breakdown on April 23. Treated psychiatrically in Montreux, Switzerland and diagnosed as schizophrenic.

1931 Zelda on way to "recovery" when death of her father broke her down again.

1932 Moved to Baltimore.

1934 Novel *Tender Is the Night,* delineating European locales and wife's mental illness, published. Relative failure financially. Creates very mixed impression upon critics and even upon his friend, since the mid-1920s, Ernest Hemingway.

1935 A collection of short stories, *Taps at Reveille,* published.

1936 Three confessional articles published in *Esquire* magazine starting with "The Crack-Up." Mother died.

1937 Signed a six-month contract with Metro-Goldwyn-Mayer in Hollywood.

1938 Moved to Malibu Beach. MGM contract not renewed.

1939 Ill-fated trip to Dartmouth to work on film scenario with Budd Schulberg. Started writing *The Last Tycoon.*

1940 Moved to Hollywood in April. Suffered first heart attack in November. Died on December 21 in the presence of his friend Sheilah Graham, the motion picture columnist. Literary revival began about a year later with the publication of his fragmentary novel *The Last Tycoon,* which was given an extraordinarily enthusiastic review by Stephen Vincent Benet in *The Saturday Review of Literature.*

INTRODUCTION

THE CHRONICLER of F. Scott Fitzgerald's career rarely fails to cast a spell like that of the ancient mariner upon his captivated audience. Three best sellers within a dozen years (by Budd Schulberg, Arthur Mizener, and Andrew Turnbull) as well as a fairly successful Broadway play, *The Disenchanted*, made out of Schulberg's novel, all testify to the power of the story of his forty-four hectic years over the imaginations of both the simple and the sophisticated, regardless of whether the tale is told as fiction or as history. Even relatively minor episodes of his life, like the one narrated by Sheilah Graham in *Beloved Infidel*, have exercised a fascination upon the minds of a fairly large and miscellaneous public in our time. And this is because, like his perennially popular fiction, his life is filled with surprisingly adventurous and romantic elements, with a deep tincture of melancholy and tragedy, a combination which few are able to resist if it is at all well told.

The prospect of the biographers' attention did not bring unmixed delight to Fitzgerald. Judging by one of the reflections which he put down in his notebooks, he was inclined to discourage their attempts: "There never was a good biography of a good novelist. There couldn't be. He's too many people if he's any good." Apparently, to him, the novelist was like the god Proteus, capable of taking any one of innumerable forms, according to his need. The creator of many characters, he was himself without definable character such as would give a spinal structure to a history of his life. Or perhaps, his idea was not unlike that expressed by Joyce in a memorable sentence in *Portrait of the Artist as a Young Man*: "The artist, like the God of the creation, remains within or behind or beyond or above his handiwork, invisible, refined out of existence, indifferent, paring his fingernails."

In another passage of his notebooks, Fitzgerald indicated that the heroes of his books—Amory Blaine (in *This Side of Paradise*), Anthony Patch (in *The Beautiful and Damned*), Jay Gatsby (in *The Great Gatsby*), Dick Diver (in *Tender Is the Night*) and

1

Monroe Stahr (in *The Last Tycoon*)—all bore a likeness to himself, like older or younger, more dissolute or integrated brothers of his own (imaginatively speaking, of course, for in reality he was an only child). The novelist apparently was engaged all his life in the experiment of transposing his autobiography to realize various potentialities which he felt swarming in himself. The subject which the writer himself was able to explore in depth with the greatest possible direct knowledge, his biographer could never hope to understand except superficially. Walt Whitman put this thought into one of his "Inscriptions" to *Leaves of Grass*:

When I read the book, the biography famous,
And is this then (said I) what the author calls a man's life?
And so will someone when I am dead and gone write my life?
(As if any man really knew aught of my life,
Why even I myself I often think know little or nothing of my real life,
Only a few hints, a few diffused faint clews and indirections
I seek for my own use to trace out here.)

Romanticism, stressing the uniqueness of each individual (every romantic writer since Rousseau has believed with the latter that if he was no better than others he was at least completely different from them and that his creator, after the job was done, threw away the mold from which he was made) and the unmatched intensity of his feelings, makes the biographer's efforts to understand another being more complicated than himself arrogant and foolhardy. Yet such reflections, paradoxically, instead of frightening biographers away, have acted as a goad and challenge to them, and the art of biography has flourished in the romantic period as never before in history.

The main outlines of Fitzgerald's life are clear enough. He was born in September 1896 in St. Paul, Minnesota, and died in December 1940 in Hollywood, California. He lived at various times in the eastern parts of the United States: Boston (where he attended the Newman Preparatory School), Princeton University, New York City, Long Island, Baltimore. He also lived in France for some time, both in Paris and on the coast of the Riviera; the first he was to describe in his story "Babylon Revisited," the second in the novel *Tender Is the Night*.

His racial background is not without significance. On his father's side, he came from an old American family (his first two names, Francis Scott, he owes to the ancestor who composed the Star

Spangled Banner); on his mother's side he came from newer and more vigorous immigrant stock. On both sides, he was descended from that greatly gifted Irish nation, which has contributed so striking a share to modern literature. It is not only names like Joyce, Yeats, and O'Neill that come to mind immediately in this connection, but also the rhythms of speech and phrasing of Irish men and women, who, unknown to fame, often make us conscious of a linguistic gift, an imagination, a sense of style, which are of the same stuff we find in their better-known countrymen. The magical charm of Fitzgerald's way with words (in this respect he outshines not only all his prose contemporaries in America but many of the poets as well) is not merely an individual attribute; it is the quintessence of a quality that seems to be shared in some degree by a substantial part of a whole people.

The legend that his father was a failure is derived primarily from Fitzgerald himself, and although many biographers concur in this, it has perhaps less basis in fact than in Fitzgerald's own need to think of himself as a completely self-made man who, like his heroes Gatsby and Monroe Stahr, apparently sprang full-blown from his own Platonic, or ideal conception of himself. When his father lost his last major business position in the east the twelve-year-old boy seems to have dwelt on the setback morbidly so that it took on the proportions of a catastrophe. This event, however, did not take place until 1908 when Mr. Fitzgerald was fifty-five years old, not an unseemly age at which to retire from the active struggle of life if only one can afford to do so. Though his retirement was not voluntary or complete, Mr. Fitzgerald was fortunately able to retire, since his wife had inherited money. When they all moved back from Buffalo to St. Paul that year, the family could live on the income from a fortune of more than $125,000, which was Mrs. Fitzgerald's legacy from her father, who had become the first "tycoon" of his family. The sum is substantial even today, and in the first decade of this century, when the uninflated dollar was worth several times what it is now, it must have been more impressive still. Fitzgerald, who liked to think of himself as a poor boy because he naturally gravitated toward friendship with much richer men, actually belonged to the same comfortable rentier class as the modern master he so much admired, Marcel Proust.

The affinity with Proust, which can be felt in the texture of some of Fitzgerald's descriptive passages, particularly in *Tender Is the Night*, extends to certain aspects of their lives as well. The biogra-

3

phers of both dwell upon their expensive tastes and their habit of giving tips to waiters that sometimes exceeded the amount of the original bill. For Fitzgerald, life would hardly have been worth living except on such a scale, and it is fortunate that he had the kind of storytelling gift which could be turned to popular uses. No matter how much he earned, he spent his money so lavishly that several times he came to the verge of bankruptcy. Proust, on the other hand, who did not have the same sort of facility and who never went out to face the world on its own economic terms, felt that life should have been perfectly tolerable even if he had been compelled to make his career as a schoolmaster in the provinces. Aside from the differences in their sexual tastes (the stubborn conventionality of one and the stubborn *un*conventionality of the other) the principal distinction between them as artists is that Fitzgerald's standing with the intellectuals was preceded by his raw appeal to the crowd of ordinary readers, while the situation was reversed in the case of Proust: the public takes him, if at all, on faith in the taste of its intellectuals.

If one could say what the heart of Fitzgerald's appeal is, it would be that in a time of general rebelliousness and breakdown of traditions and a worship of youth by America, Fitzgerald was himself the greatest worshiper of youth and the defender of its standards— or the lack of them. Turnbull quotes a letter which he wrote to his cousin Ceci during World War I: "Life hasn't much to offer except youth, and for older people the love of youth in others." Undoubtedly, his desire to shock in part accounts for the expression of such sentiments, and yet one feels that he must have believed basically in the truth of what he was saying. He seems to have regarded himself at times as like the naive child who dares to discover the nakedness of accepted moral views. His bravado and nihilism were too consistent to admit of any other interpretation.

In *The Great Gatsby* he defined personality as "an unbroken series of successful gestures." In the sense that his own verbal gestures were certainly consistent, he was a successful personality. In him, it is nearly impossible to separate flamboyance from sincerity. He rejected wisdom, moderation, and restraint as ideals of human conduct. When we consider his ultimate fate, there seems something more than mere boyishness or Byronism in a letter to his editor Maxwell Perkins in which he says: "I should like to sit down with half a dozen chosen companions and drink myself to death, but I am sick alike of life, liquor, and literature."

Ripeness and maturity to Fitzgerald appear to have been synonymous with rottenness. He should hardly have understood, let alone sympathized with, the famous statement of Sophocles—which Plato quotes with approval—that he welcomed old age because it was freeing him from his passions. Fitzgerald was one of those for whom, as Socrates remarks in *The Apology,* the philosophic life was not worth living. Against the wisdom of the ages, he posited the wisdom of his own age, which may be defined as that of a shallow and perennial youthfulness. In art, too, he drew the logical consequences of the same unsound assumptions. Against the ideas of Aristotle who commends the probable and the representative as the fittest subject matter for the dramatic writer, Fitzgerald advises us in his notebooks that "reporting the extreme things as if they were the average things will start you on the art of fiction."

In short, Fitzgerald was part of a second great wave of romanticism in the world within a century, and, far from having learned anything from the bitter experience of his predecessors, he went in some respects to greater lengths than they did in defying reason and good sense. Santayana is often quoted to the effect that those who will not learn from history are condemned to repeat it. But observing examples like Fitzgerald, one would have to think that the lesson most clearly taught is that we are often condemned (by ourselves perhaps) to repeat history compulsively. The new romantics in the twentieth century tried not only to emulate the vagaries of their melancholy predecessors but to go far beyond them. Even his wife Zelda, who could hardly have been called a classicist, remarked in a letter to Perkins from Europe: "Scott reads nothing but lives of Byron and Shelley and shows the most romantic proclivities." When his mother dared to give him some moralistic advice, he rudely rejected it by saying that her precepts were suited to someone whose aim in life was to become "chief clerk at fifty" but would hardly do for a liberated spirit like himself.

The pernicious effects of romantic theory upon Fitzgerald's colorful life have been well documented (generally sympathetically) by his various biographers. The ideals of balance, equilibrium, and equanimity held no attraction whatsoever for Fitzgerald. Or, let us rather say, they were not for him as a person, though the moral axioms upon which conduct must be founded may sometimes be deduced from the events in his fictions, because they arise out of human nature itself. That Fitzgerald himself may have recognized that he sometimes wrote more wisely than he lived is shown by his

5

quaint confession that he occasionally read over his own books in search of advice as to how to handle his problems!

The tales of the capers in which he indulged are partially responsible for the popularity of his biographies. It is entertaining to be told of such antics, though it might have inspired very different feelings if one were forced to become involved in them. Some of the unpleasant realities transpire through Turnbull's sympathetic descriptions:

> Around New York he remained the incorrigible undergraduate. He and Zelda surrendered to impulses which wouldn't even have occurred to more prosaic souls. The two of them taking hands after a Carnegie Hall concert and running like the wind—like two young hawks—down crowded 57th Street, in and out of traffic. Scott doing handstands in the Biltmore lobby because he hadn't been in the news that week, and, as Oscar Wilde said, the only thing worse than being talked about is being forgotten. Scott and Zelda at the theater sitting quietly during the funny parts and roaring when the house was still. Scott whimsically divesting himself of coat, vest, and shirt in the sixth row of the *Scandals,* and being helped out by a posse of ushers. Scott and Zelda going to a party, one of them on the roof of the car and the other on the hood.

The life of the Fitzgeralds in France was even more sensational:

> (Scott) wanted each evening to be adventurous, spectacular, unpredictable, and when nothing happened, as was usually the case, he either fell asleep or made a scene . . . Once when (he and Zelda and the Murphys) were driving to Les Halles, Fitzgerald, who hadn't much use for the color of the old market, created a little color of his own by chewing hundred franc notes (the equivalent of twenty dollar bills) and spitting them out the taxi window. "Oh Scott, they're so dirty," Sara protested, but Fitzgerald went right on. Finally the driver could stand it no longer. Stopping the cab, he ran back to retrieve some of the money. Fitzgerald jumped into the driver's seat and headed for the Seine, saying he was going to plunge them into it. As he came to one of the ramps, they managed to get the wheel away from him and return it to the terrified driver, who came flapping up behind them in his long coat.

Of such stories, there is an embarrassment of riches in his biography even for the most jaded appetites. Some of them are funny, many are simply sad and dispiriting, others are positively alarming.

Long before she had to be institutionalized, Zelda was giving definite indications that she was profoundly disturbed. Hemingway, we know, was convinced she was crazy the first time he met her.

Fitzgerald and his wife would have been difficult enough apart from each other; together, they were impossible. He was truly witty, and she (to borrow Melville's description of the cabin boy, Pip, in *Moby Dick*) was crazy-witty. Each seems to have brought out the worst weaknesses of the other and at the same time created an illusion of social acceptance and a feeling of rapport where none really existed. Turnbull tersely captures the essence of this unlucky combination in a striking simile: "It is hard to say whether he or she was the leader in this chaos. They complemented each other like gin and vermouth in a martini, each making the other more powerful in their war with dullness and convention."

Other people—even the most imperceptive—could see that the Fitzgeralds were headed for disaster but were unable to do anything to help the gifted, tragic pair whose actions they were watching. This frustration was felt even by those friends in their own generation who had not yet been completely unhinged by speed, war, alcohol, and the violent break with tradition, religion, and ethics to which these led. The actress Laurette Taylor is quoted as having said to her husband on returning from a Fitzgerald party: "I've just seen the doom of youth. A walking doom!"

All his life, Fitzgerald seems to have labored under the romantic fallacy implicit in an offhand remark which was recorded by his secretary: "People are divided into two classes. There are those who think, are sensitive, and have some fatal flaw. Then there are those who are good and unimaginative—and uninteresting." Yet there is some evidence that he did appreciate at times the solid values of traditional ethics and desired to be thought, in the last analysis, to possess them. In this connection, a story told about himself and his father-in-law is pathetically instructive. It is clear that Zelda's father, a judge in the Alabama Supreme Court, was not happy with his daughter's choice of a husband. He is quoted by Turnbull as saying once to his daughter: "I think you better divorce him—you can't really make a life with a fella like that." When Zelda objected that Scott was the best person in the world when he was sober, her father replied bitterly: "He's never sober." It was before this forbidding figure that Fitzgerald is said to have gone down on his knees on one occasion and asked for the equivalent of blessing and reassurance. "Tell me you believe in me," he pleaded. But the judge refused him any comfort and said with disarming irony: "I think you will always pay your bills."

His father-in-law's words proved prophetic, particularly about the latter half of Fitzgerald's life. In his spendthrift youth, he felt, like certain other Americans of his time (Mayor James J. Walker of New York was a flagrant example), that it was degrading to live within the limits of his income (see, for example, his facetious advice to his contemporaries in his 1924 article on "How To Live on $36,000 a Year"). Despite the fact that the "bills" for the reckless expenditures of his earlier life kept mounting to dizzying heights— for his wife's hospitalization in private mental institutions, for his daughter's education at Vassar, for his own considerable medical and nursing needs, and for the upkeep of a Hollywood establishment—he managed at the end to pay off long standing debts to his agent Harold Ober and to others. Somewhat miraculously, he avoided insolvency and even put away what Whitman once called "a little burial money."

He was able to do this though he was no longer a popular author during his last years. The secret of his unusual solvency at the end of his life lay in his very substantial income in Hollywood, and one must balance carefully his real grievances, aesthetic and moral, against the film makers with the fact that financially he should have been much worse off but for their willingness to pay him as much as $1500 a week largely on the strength of his reputation rather than his present usefulness to them. Thus he was able to save what was, for him, an incredible amount of his earnings and to use it conscientiously to repay his debts and to support his loved ones, particularly his daughter, in the style to which he had accustomed them. His last years revealed a saving grace and a fundamental sense of decency, which prevented him from leaving the world in a state of bankruptcy, material as well as spiritual. He applied his restraining brakes too late to avoid the crash, but in his sufferings he certainly showed that he possessed an exacting and almost puritanical "inner check."

His final years, like his earlier ones, are, of course, filled with contradictions. As with every romantic, beginning with Rousseau, Fitzgerald's head and heart at times seem not to belong to the same person. Sheilah Graham's memoir, *Beloved Infidel,* shows him in postures, in his last days, as unattractive as any of those during his youth. In Miss Graham's description, he was drunk, dissolute, and dangerous during a quite sizable proportion of the time in which she knew him. One can understand why she should have felt her life threatened by him, and, on at least one occasion, she called upon the police to intervene.

Nevertheless, a struggle was raging within Fitzgerald to amend his own conduct and the bad habits that had grown to be stronger than he was, as is evident from the letters during his later years, particularly those he wrote to his daughter. In them the pose of the youthful and flaming rebel, which he had cultivated for so long, is replaced by that of a man determined to succeed in becoming conventional, even strait-laced. Ironically enough, the tone he assumed toward his child is similar to the one his mother had used toward him, and one which he had cruelly derided. He warns his daughter, for example, against precisely the sort of snobbery to which he had himself succumbed at her age. He cautions her to restrain her impulses with a prudence that he might once have regarded as bourgeois if not cowardly (for example, he tells her not to write any anti-Semitic remarks on postcards lest—the period being the late 1930s—they both be mistaken for partisans of the unspeakable Nazis). He cannot seem to understand why she willfully insists upon repeating her parents' mistakes when she has them before her eyes as horrible examples of how life is *not* to be lived. The same question could have been asked of himself once and of everyone else who is growing up. The moral law, like the moon, has to be personally discovered again by every generation. He never allowed himself to realize, however, that the most powerful teaching of which parents are capable is the setting of a good example for their children. His own example, more frequently than not, was deplorable, but he takes the attitude, which is really too easy to assume: "Do not do as I do, but as I say!" Words never came to him cheaply when he sat down to write, though it must be said that in his most creative phase he had shied away in his novels from the kind of cant which crept into his tone when he wrote to his daughter. The advice he gives her is good, but one wishes that it were not so much at variance with the way he was living at the time. Some of the scenes described by Miss Graham in her book seem to be almost psychopathic in origin. One concludes, after examining the evidence, that when it came to his art he was a master; when it came to the conduct of his life, he was a failure. The price he paid for the contempt he had for the safe-and-sane conventional individual is that he never quite succeeded in becoming one himself. In certain circles, this very inadequacy has made him a hero, and even in his own eyes he continued to speak with what he romantically termed "the authority of failure."

What Fitzgerald once wrote about one of the most obnoxious characters he ever created, Tom Buchanan in *The Great Gatsby,* may, unfortunately, be just as true of himself. The football player Buchanan, during his sensational career at Yale, had become "a national figure in a way, one of those men who reach such an acute limited excellence at twenty-one that everything afterwards savors of anticlimax." The career of Fitzgerald himself might be described as an experiment designed to find out what would have become of a number of romantic poets who had died young and seemingly before they had had a chance to realize their promise. If we may judge by Fitzgerald's case, the world apparently did not lose very much artistically in their untimely departure.

The climax of Fitzgerald's literary career came when he was nearer thirty than twenty, in 1925 and 1926 when he was publishing *The Great Gatsby* and "The Rich Boy." "Acute limited excellence" describes the quality of his own accomplishment very well. He was always conscious of his limitations and consoled himself for them by comparing himself in his letters not to what was just as excellent and less limited but to what was not excellent at all. In *Gatsby,* he speaks of "that most limited of specialists, the 'well-rounded man.' This isn't just an epigram—life is much more successfully looked at from a single window, after all."

The awareness of his own abrupt decline is what lies behind such well-known self-descriptive statements as the one in his notebooks in which he observes that "there are no second acts in American lives." However, in an overwhelming number of ways, despite the boast of self-knowledge which he had made in the conclusion of *This Side of Paradise,* Fitzgerald quite obviously did not know himself. This is one of the sources of his eventual discomfiture—the word "failure" which Fitzgerald used in describing himself is probably too melodramatic to be completely accurate. But his courageous acceptance of the best-informed estimates of his general decline and the anticlimactic nature of his career is justified by the cold facts. The attempts by some biographers to deny these facts is a result of their own romanticism.

The "acute limited excellence" of Fitzgerald expressed itself most lastingly in the form of the novel. "The novel," Fitzgerald wrote in his memoir *The Crack-Up*, "at my maturity was the strongest and supplest medium for conveying thought and emotion from one human being to another." It was fortunate for his own prosperity that he felt this way, for if there is one form of literature that is by far the most popular in the modern world, it is the novel. Despite the inroads that motion pictures, television, and picture magazines have made on whatever free time is left over from the perusal of the daily newspaper and the current periodicals, viable novels still find readers.

The novel has been so strongly identified with the spirit of modernity that a man like Irving Babbitt, reacting sharply against romanticism in general, has expressed his disapproval of this literary form. In his book, *The New Laoköon*, Babbitt mounted a powerful attack upon the novel, which deserves more attention than it has received:

> The novel is the one genre that . . . (has) no formal limits, and so was admirably adapted, as Rousseau showed in the "Nouvelle Héloise," to free emotional expansion. The novel is not only the least purposeful of literary forms, the one that lends itself most naturally to all the meanders of feeling, to a vast overflow of "soul" in the romantic sense, but it also admits most readily a photographic realism,—that is, an art without selection. The triumph of the novel has been, if not the triumph of formlessness over form, at least the triumph of diffuseness over concentration. Friedrich Schlegel was right from his own point of view in exalting the novel as a sort of confusion of all the other literary forms, the visible embodiment of that chaos of human nature of which he dreamed.

Babbitt probably has in mind Schlegel's extravagant claims on behalf of the novel as the modern equivalent of the Socratic dialogue. "In this free form," wrote Schlegel, "the wisdom which has fled from the philosophers has found a refuge." Such statements were calculated to arouse the polemical zeal of Irving Babbitt. Babbitt's position finds unexpected support in an unlikely quarter —from a man who was himself a highly successful, popular novelist. Arnold Bennett, in a little book called *How To Live on Twenty-Fours Hours a Day*, suggests a budget of leisure time for the man of business, and this budget includes three sessions a week of an hour and a half each devoted to what he calls "serious reading." In connection with this, he makes the observation:

Novels are excluded from the "serious reading" of 90 minutes three times a week—for the reason that bad novels ought not to be read, and that good novels never demand any appreciable mental application on the part of the readers. A good novel rushes you forward like a skiff down a stream, and you arrive at the end, perhaps breathless, but unexhausted. The best novels involve the least strain. Now in the cultivation of the mind one of the most important factors is precisely the feeling of strain, of difficulty, of a task which one part of you is anxious to achieve and another part of you is anxious to shirk, and that feeling cannot be got in facing a novel.

Bennett is not being ironic; what he says deserves serious consideration. The first objection that occurs to us is that there may be a difficulty in reading associated simply with the novelty or complication of the author's technique. No one would maintain that Joyce's *Ulysses* and still less *Finnegan's Wake* are not good novels because they do not "rush you forward like a skiff down a stream." Proust's *Remembrance* and even a work like Mann's *Magic Mountain* present us with similar difficulties. If it is the feeling of intellectual strain that one is seeking, one could do worse than to tackle such works. But perhaps this is not what Bennett means. It is true in a sense that even the greatest masterpieces of the art of the novel—Dostoevski's *The Brothers Karamazov* and Tolstoi's *War and Peace*—are intended to be comparatively easy reading.

The challenge begins not in reading such books but in rereading them. What Thomas Mann once said of *The Magic Mountain* in a lecture at Princeton is applicable to other examples of this literary form:

What is there that I can say about the book . . . and the best way to read it? I shall begin with a very arrogant request that it be read not once but twice. A request not to be heeded, of course, if one has been bored at first reading. A work of art must not be a task or an effort; it must not be undertaken against one's will. It is meant to give pleasure, to entertain and enliven. If it does not have this effect on a reader, he must put it down and turn to something else. But if you have read *The Magic Mountain* once, I recommend that you read it twice. The way in which a book is composed results in the reader's getting a deeper enjoyment from the second reading. Just as in music one needs to know a piece to enjoy it properly.

12

When the matter is viewed in this light, we see that Bennett's observations are only partially true. What Fitzgerald once said about a lyric poem like Keats's "Ode on a Grecian Urn" may be translated so as to apply to the novel as well: "I suppose I've read it a hundred times. About the tenth time I began to know what it was about, and caught the chime in it and the exquisite inner mechanics." One cannot, of course, read a sizable novel as often as one can read a fifty-line poem, but the prose does not yield its secrets, particularly the secrets of its form, more readily than does the poem. It begins by appealing to our curiosity but ends by inviting our reflection. The superficial appearance of the novel may be trivial and unimpressive, but in the best examples of the art there is much that is problematical and even profound.

If it is possible to understand what gave rise to the reaction against the novel on the part of men like Irving Babbitt, it is also at times possible to sympathize with the enthusiasm for it expressed by a man like Ludwig Lewisohn in his book, *Expression in America.* A practising novelist himself, Lewisohn wrote:

Of all the forms of expression invented by man the modern novel —the novel that began with Henry Fielding and culminates for this year and decade with Thomas Mann—is the most various and the most powerful, capable at once of the noblest breadth and the deepest intimacy, apt at the expression of all moods and impulses and ideas, of all conflicts whether between man and man or between the individual and society, more purging than the briefer shock of tragedy, more illuminating to average men and women than the difficult treatises of philosophers, enlarging experience, cleansing vision, bringing home to the obdurate bosom characters and fates differing from its own and thus serving the cause of understanding and tolerance and peace among men. If the history of the later literature of America is so largely the history of its novelists and novels it is because everywhere and not least among us the novel has absorbed into itself the functions of the other and older kinds and is to the majority of men drama and poetry, epic and treatise.

The highest tribute to Fitzgerald that one can render is to say that at his best he seems to be worthy of celebration with some such rhetoric as this.

A contemporary critic, noted for the perversity of his paradoxes rather than for their profundity, has said that the fascination of

F. Scott Fitzgerald

Fitzgerald's literary accomplishments is inseparable from that exercised by the legend of his life. My own feeling, on the contrary, is that the legend is an obscuring mist between the reader and everything that is most charming in his work. The comparison which this critic suggested between Fitzgerald and Byron seems inept, if only because there is nothing coarse about Fitzgerald's handling of the English language as there occasionally is about Byron's work (Matthew Arnold was probably the first to point this out in an essay which was a strong defense nevertheless of Byron's genius).

If comparisons are in order at all, one with John Keats is more apt. There is something as profoundly poetic at times about Fitzgerald's use of language as there is about Keats's. This quality is apparently imperceptible to those not native to English. The results are not dissimilar in both cases. In the nineteenth century, Englishmen who were unduly awed by Byron's European fame and success with men as great as Goethe and Taine were inclined to overestimate his stature in spite of their distinct feelings of occasional linguistic lapses in his work. In our own time, Hemingway and Faulkner, who have been appreciated by Gide, Sartre, and other influential European literary figures, may have been given a little more than their due on this account by their intellectual countrymen as compared with Fitzgerald. There is an insuperable difficulty in communicating the excellence of a style to a foreigner who, at best, sees it as through a glass darkly. That is why the reputations of writers with their own people is so often different from what it is with other peoples.

The best apology for what has been called "the notorious irregularity of Fitzgerald's life" is probably the one contained in lines addressed by the poet Auden to Yeats at the time of the latter's death:

> Time that is intolerant
> Of the brave and innocent . . .
> Worships language and forgives
> Everyone by whom it lives.

In his blackest moments of quite justified despair, Fitzgerald denied both innocence and bravery to himself, and in truth the spectacle presented by his life was often a sorry one. But if he did not have command over himself at all times, he never failed with regard to the English language which he loved. On that score, his confidence never

14

deserted him, and an ever increasing number of readers have agreed that it was well founded. Gertrude Stein proved to be a prophetic critic when she said in 1933: "Fitzgerald will be read when many of his well-known contemporaries are forgotten."

THIS SIDE OF PARADISE

"Every real novelist . . . is, at bottom, a moralist."

W. H. Auden

IN A SYMPOSIUM in 1930 on Babbitt's and More's Humanism, edited by C. Hartley Grattan, John Chamberlain, summing up the accomplishments and shortcomings of the preceding decade in the field of fiction, wrote:

> We had the definitely nonphilosophical novel. *This Side of Paradise,* which remains the most charming novel of the time, was wholly non-philosophical; it was a record of sensations; and ideas, when present in it, were treated more or less as delightful playthings. Our artists were very much wrapped up with problems of personality that were distinct from social problems. Amory Blaine, for example, ended by saying: "I know myself, but that is all." An individual was an individual, not a member of a community, a society, a nation, a world. Society was something to be shunned.

This criticism may serve as a point of departure. It is not that Fitzgerald's first book contained no philosophy or ideas; rather, in retrospect, it seems that its philosophy and ideas are threadbare and inadequate. The sentence quoted by Chamberlain, which is the concluding affirmation of *This Side of Paradise,* is a good example of this inadequacy. "I know myself, but that is all." That is a hollow boast; it is precisely what the author himself in an earlier section of his novel had described as "an ostensible epigram." He had remarked that the coinage of such simulacra of sophistication was not the hardest intellectual feat possible. It is his tribute of imitation to the witticisms of Oscar Wilde which he admired inordinately in his days as a Princeton undergraduate.

Fitzgerald delighted in experimenting with words during this period just to see what would happen when familiar truths were reversed. In this glittering sentence he implies that what Socrates and the Delphic oracle had taken to be the most difficult problem set by human life—namely, self-knowledge—is really not so difficult an achievement and, moreover, is a mere introduction to the serious business of life. As a mature and sober conclusion rather than as a paradox, this ending of the book wilts under scrutiny. It does not even stand up against the well-known conclusion of Joyce's *Portrait of the Artist as a Young Man*: "I go to encounter for the millionth time the reality of experience and to forge in the smithy of my soul the uncreated conscience of my race."

Joyce's sentence, too, is somewhat vitiated by its inflated romantic rhetoric, and it is more impressive on first reading than it is later on, yet it does contain some real thought and genuine feeling. Fitzgerald's epigram, by comparison, only attests to his cleverness in the manipulation of words, which contain little or no significant content. He wished to dazzle the reader, not to enlighten him, and he succeeded far beyond his expectations. More than 50,000 American readers were dazzled by his brilliance when the book was published in 1920, and it was a far more impressive success than he scored with his genuine masterpiece, *The Great Gatsby,* five years later.

This Side of Paradise is at the same time a better book and a poorer one than Chamberlain has said. Its principal defect is one which it shares with Fitzgerald's unfinished novel about Hollywood, *The Last Tycoon.* He assumes that his reader is interested in the purely "social" side of his subject apart from its human values, and he sets out consequently to compose (in part) a guidebook—to Princeton or to the secret life of the Hollywood studios—which will satisfy a form of vulgar curiosity. The novel that subordinates drama and story in order to serve as a sociological guidebook is on the same level with the scandalous *roman à clef.* In both, if we may draw analogy between art and the academic life, the extracurricular activities have usurped the place of the educational curriculum.

I do not mean to suggest that Fitzgerald is telling merely an "inside story" of the affluent youth of Princeton or that he completely neglects the novelist's legitimate concerns, but in proportion to the novel as a whole there is altogether too much attention given to what Fitzgerald himself calls "the breathless social system" of a leading American university. Snobbery can, of course, be objectively dissected (as it is, for example, in much of Proust's work) with profit as well as pleasure for the reader. But the author of *This Side of Paradise* did not penetrate into his material deeply enough to succeed in doing this. The result is that the exposure of the meretriciousness of Princeton's "breathless social system" is not very convincing although its presentation is colorful and superficially attractive.

We are treated to a "confidential" view of the true facts about undergraduate life:

> From the first he loved Princeton—its lazy beauty, its half-grasped significance, the wild moonlight revel of the rushes, the handsome, prosperous big-game crowds, and under it all the air of struggle that pervaded his class. From the day when, wild-eyed and exhausted, the jerseyed freshmen sat in the gymnasium and elected someone from Hill School class president, a Lawrenceville celebrity vice-president, a hockey-star from St. Paul's secretary, up until the end of the sophomore year it never ceased . . . First it was schools, and Amory, alone from St. Regis', watched the crowds form and widen and form again; St. Paul's, Hill, Pomfret, eating at certain tacitly reserved tables in Commons, dressing in their own corners of the gymnasium, and drawing unconsciously about them a barrier of the slightly less important but socially ambitious to protect them from the friendly, rather puzzled high-school element . . .

There is a good deal of amusing, if not very profound, analysis of this sort in the book—for example, the contrast that is drawn up in parallel columns between the prep school "Slicker" and "The Big Man"—which shows the author's shrewd eye for social types. There is also the edifying, editorial tone that he takes toward such post World War I phenomena as "the petting party": here, he turns his attention for a moment away from the young in his audience, who are his primary target and concern (he takes the tone toward them of one who would serve as their "guide, philosopher, and friend" in penetrating the mysterious world of Princeton and its environs), in the direction of parents in the older generation. To this latter audience he exposes the seamy side of the life of his generation—or rather the form taken by juvenile delinquency in that particular postwar period:

> None of the Victorian mothers—and most of the mothers were Victorian—had any idea how casually their daughters were accustomed to be kissed. "Servant girls are that way," says Mrs. Huston Carmelite to her popular daughter. "They are kissed first and proposed to afterward." . . . Amory saw girls doing things that even in his memory would have been impossible: eating three o'clock, after-

19

dance suppers in impossible cafes, talking of every side of life with an air half of earnestness, half of mockery, yet with a furtive excitement that Amory considered stood for a real moral let-down. But he never realized how widespread it was until he saw the cities between New York and Chicago as one vast juvenile intrigue.

But the real heart of the book into which Fitzgerald pours the best of his youthful romanticism is to be found in those passages in which he idealizes Princeton and all it stands for:

The night mist fell. From the moon it rolled, clustered about the spires and towers, and then settled below them, so that the dreaming peaks were still in lofty aspiration toward the sky. Figures that dotted the day like ants now brushed along as shadowy ghosts, in and out of the foreground. The Gothic halls and cloisters were infinitely more mysterious as they loomed suddenly out of the darkness, outlined each by myriad faint squares of yellow light. Indefinitely from somewhere a bell boomed the quarter-hour, and Amory, pausing by the sun-dial, stretched himself out on the grass. The cool bathed his eyes and slowed the flight of time—time that had crept so insidiously through the lazy April afternoons, seemed so intangible in the long spring twilights. Evening after evening the senior singing had drifted over the campus in melancholy beauty, and through the shell of his undergraduate consciousness had broken a deep and reverent devotion to the gray walls and Gothic peaks and all symbolized as warehouses of dead ages . . . . The college dreamed on— awake. He felt a nervous excitement that might have been the very throb of its slow heart . . .

The vocabulary, as well as the ideas in this passage, recalls to mind the famous address of Matthew Arnold to Oxford University in the preface to his Essays:

Adorable dreamer, whose heart has been so romantic! who hast given thyself so prodigally, given thyself to sides and to heroes not mine, only never to the Philistines! home of lost causes, and forsaken beliefs, and unpopular names, and impossible loyalties! what example could ever so inspire us to keep down the Philistine in ourselves . . . . Apparitions of a day, what is our puny warfare against the Philistines, compared with the warfare which this queen of romance has been waging against them for centuries, and will wage after we are gone?

One great difference between Arnold's Oxford and Fitzgerald's Princeton, however, is that the former, despite its fragrant bouquet of romanticism, is a potent symbol of humane tradition for which a mature man had fought the good fight all his life, while the latter is emblematic only of immature rebelliousness and even perversity in the face of all conventionally accepted ideas. To put it more bluntly, Arnold's Oxford is capable of serving as a man's ideal, but Fitzgerald's Princeton is the creation of a precocious boy's mind. When Arnold calls his university "home of lost causes and forsaken beliefs" there is a ring of nobility in the words, but comparable sentiments in Fitzgerald only succeed in sounding a trifle silly and affected. One of the hero's conversations with Monsignor Darcy, for instance, goes like this:

"I was for Bonnie Prince Charlie," announced Amory.
"Of course you were—and for Hannibal—"
"Yes, and for the Southern Confederacy." He was rather skeptical about being an Irish patriot—he suspected that being Irish was being somewhat common—but Monsignor assured him that Ireland was a romantic lost cause and Irish people quite charming, and that it should, by all means be one of his principal biases.

Later on, when Amory grows more conscious and self-critical, he realizes vividly the futility and meaninglessness of such enthusiasms:

He was not even a Catholic, yet that was the only ghost of a code that he had, the gaudy, ritualistic, paradoxical Catholicism whose prophet was Chesterton, whose claqueurs were such reformed rakes of literateurs as Huysmans and Bourget, whose American sponsor was Ralph Adams Cram, with his adulation of thirteenth century cathedrals—a Catholicism which Amory found convenient and ready-made, without priests or sacraments, or sacrifice.

Like Proust, Fitzgerald from the beginning was searching for a home-grown aristocracy, and in twentieth-century America he was bound to be even less successful in this search than was the French writer. He found only a semblance of the real thing in the class which, in a well-known conversation with Hemingway, he called "the very rich." But much of his creative effort is directed to depicting his disillusion with the simulacrum and to demonstrating its

21

inadequacy in fulfilling the demands of his romantic imagination. There is, for example, in *This Side of Paradise* the striking portrait of Dick Humbird:

> Dick Humbird had, ever since freshman year, seemed to Amory a perfect type of aristocrat. He was slender but well-built—black curly hair, straight features, and rather a dark skin. Everything he said sounded intangibly appropriate. He possessed infinite courage, an averagely good mind, and a sense of honor with a clear charm and noblesse oblige that varied it from righteousness. He could dissipate without going to pieces, and even his most bohemian adventures never seemed "running it out." People dressed like him, tried to talk as he did . . . He differed from the healthy type that was essentially middle-class—he never seemed to perspire. Some people couldn't be familiar with a chauffeur without having it returned; Humbird could have lunched at Sherry's with a colored man, yet people would have somehow known that it was all right. He was not a snob, though he knew only half his class. His friends ranged from the highest to the lowest, but it was impossible to "cultivate" him. Servants worshipped him, and treated him like a god. He seemed the eternal example of what the upper class tried to be.
>
> "He's like those pictures in the *Illustrated London News* of the . English officers who have been killed," Amory had said to Alec.
>
> "Well," Alec had answered, "if you want to know the shocking truth, his father was a grocery clerk who made a fortune in Tacoma real estate and came to New York ten years ago."

In other words, Dick Humbird is more a "self-made" aristocrat than any character in Proust. In Proust, it is true that there is a distinction made between the true, hereditary aristocracy of the Faubourg Saint-Germain and those upper middle-class *arrivistes* who aspire to belong to society and eventually succeed perhaps in becoming an integral part of it. But there is a vast gulf between men such as Swann and Humbird. Swann, the son and grandson of Jewish stockbroker millionaires, is more genuinely aristocratic in his manner than the Duke of Guermantes. In this respect he resembles Humbird. The difference is that Swann's career is furthered not only by his genuinely exquisite aesthetic taste but by the long foreground of family prosperity and leisure which his American counterpart, elevated to dizzy heights by sudden wealth, entirely lacks.

One of the best aesthetic touches in this first novel of Fitzgerald, incidentally, centers around the character Humbird. As if to match the disintegration of the narrator's illusions concerning his aristocracy, there follows shortly an account of a gruesome automobile accident in which a number of Princeton boys are killed—including Humbird. Amory describes his erstwhile (and now slightly tarnished) idol as he appears in death:

> The brow was cold but the face not expressionless. He looked at the shoe-laces. Dick had tied them that morning. He had tied them—and now he was this heavy white mass. All that remained of the charm and personality of the Dick Humbird he had known—oh, it was all so horrible and unaristocratic and close to earth. All tragedy has that strain of the grotesque and squalid—so useless, futile . . . the way animals die. . . . Amory was reminded of a cat that had lain horribly mangled in some alley of his childhood.

There seems to be something, especially in the concluding sentences of the passage, of that nihilistic feeling of despair which was to find expression in his description, nearly a generation later, of his own "crack-up" and how life, then, appeared to him to be a meaningless trajectory between nothingness and nothingness. This passage and one other in which there is a description of Amory's drunken "hallucinations" (the word is put in quotes because Fitzgerald apparently intends to leave a purposeful ambiguity as to whether the supernatural is really involved—just as Hawthorne and Dostoevski do in similar scenes) concerning the Devil are the most powerful writing of the book, the clearest demonstration of the author's strength of imagination, and the surest promise of better things to come in the future. *This Side of Paradise* is the book of a writer with a long way to go in his creative career, but one who is undoubtedly engaged in getting there.

One of the prime feelings in all of Fitzgerald's work is that inspired by the contrast between wealth and poverty which America presents. He is not only attracted by the leisurely and aesthetic life which is possible for the rich but he is repelled by the ugly conditions of life to which the poor are condemned. The life of the poor is painted partly from experience and partly from imagination in *This Side of Paradise*; it is similar to the description of certain aspects of urban life in T. S. Eliot's *Preludes*:

> The rain gave Amory a feeling of detachment, and the numerous unpleasant aspects of city life without money occurred to him in threatening procession. There was the ghastly, stinking crush of the

23

subway—the car-cards thrusting themselves at one, leering out like dull bores who grab your arm with another story; the querulous worry as to whether some one isn't leaning on you; a man deciding not to give his seat to a woman, hating her for it; the woman hating him for not doing it; at worst a squalid phantasmagoria of breath, and old cloth on human bodies and the smells of the food men ate— at best just people—too hot or too cold, tired, worried.

He pictured the rooms where these people lived—where the patterns of the blistered wall-papers were heavy reiterated sunflowers on green and yellow backgrounds, where there were tin bathtubs and gloomy hallways and verdureless, unnamable spaces in back of the buildings; where even love dressed as seduction—a sordid murder around the corner, illicit motherhood in the flat above. And always there was the economical stuffiness of indoor winter, and the long summers, nightmares of perspiration between sticky enveloping walls . . . dirty restaurants where careless, tired people helped themselves to sugar with their own used coffee-spoons, leaving hard brown deposits in the bowl . . . .

In sharp contrast with this is Fitzgerald's picture in *The Beautiful and Damned* of an opening night at a theater in the same city:

In the foyer of the theater they waited a few moments to see the first-night crowd come in. There were opera cloaks stitched of myriad, many-colored silks and furs; there were jewels dripping from arms and throats and ear-tips of white and rose; there were innumerable broad shimmers down the middles of innumerable silk hats; there were shoes of gold and bronze and red and shining black; there were the high-piled, tight packed coiffures of many women and the slick, watered hair of well-kept men—most of all there was the ebbing, flowing, chattering, chuckling, foaming, slow-rolling wave of this cheerful sea of people as to-night it poured its glittering torrent into the artificial lake of laughter.

Along with his feeling for the sheer aesthetic attractiveness of the life of the rich there is in Fitzgerald's first novel as there was to be in his later books, a profound resentment of the privileged wealthy class in America. In *This Side of Paradise,* this resentment is expressed in a number of ways—for example, in the quasi-socialist or anarchist views that Amory expounds so volubly in the closing section of the book. But it shows through most obviously in the account of the principal love affair of the book, that of Amory and Rosalind. This affair is destined from the beginning to destruction by the cold facts of economics. When Rosalind tells her mother that Amory "has a little income—and you know he's earning thirty-five dollars a week in advertising," Mrs. Connage replies dryly: "And it wouldn't buy your clothes. I have your best interests at heart when I tell you not to take a step you'll spend your days regretting."

Amory's rival is Dawson Ryder, and Rosalind, who quickly comes to share her mother's opinion as to the sensible thing to do in the situation, says of him: "He's so reliable, I almost feel that he'd be a background." A financial background of the kind he offers is, of course, essential to a girl who confesses: "I like sunshine and pretty things and cheerfulness and I dread responsibility. I don't want to think about pots and kitchens and brooms. I want to worry whether my legs will get slick and brown when I swim in the summer."

The portrayal of Rosalind and her milieu is rather cruel, and Fitzgerald in *The Crack-Up*, explained this and much of the satire in his work by revealing the deep despair into which he, like his first hero Amory, had been thrown by his financial situation at the time he was writing *This Side of Paradise*:

> It was one of those tragic loves doomed for lack of money, and one day the girl closed it out on the basis of common sense. During a long summer of despair I wrote a novel instead of letters, so it came out all right, but it came out all right for a different person. The man with the jingle of money in his pocket who married the girl a year later would always cherish an abiding distrust, an animosity toward the leisure class—not the conviction of a revolutionist but the smoldering hatred of a peasant. In the years since then I have never been able to stop wondering where my friends' money came from, nor to stop thinking that at one time a sort of *droit de seigneur* might have been exercised to give one of them my girl.

This is a melodramatically heightened formulation of the case—as is much of the writing in *The Crack-Up*—but basically it is a sound analysis of the sort of motivations that seem evident enough in his books.

Of the qualities that were to distinguish Fitzgerald's work in the years to come, the one most markedly present in his first book, as might be expected perhaps, is the style, which even then was famous. The source of Fitzgerald's poetry, like that of Keats whom he so much admired, is in his passionate concern with the present moment. The romantic poet, to quote Shelley's "Skylark," is not one who likes to look "before and after." He immerses himself in the flow of an eternal present, and it is from this surrender that he derives his power to describe the sensuous forms of the world about him. As Fitzgerald himself was to write apologetically in *The Crack-Up*:

> After all, any given moment has its value; it can be questioned in the light of afterevents, but the moment remains. The young prince in velvet gathered in lovely domesticity around the queen amid the hush of rich draperies may grow up to be Pedro the Cruel or Charles the Mad, but the moment of beauty was there.

Or, as he puts it in another place in the same book: "To record one must be unwary." In *This Side of Paradise*, as in Proust's early work *Les plaisirs et les jours*, the least debatable excellence exhibited by the author is in his style.

2

THE BEAUTIFUL AND DAMNED

FROM THE POINT OF VIEW of literary form, *The Beautiful and Damned* is probably the weakest of Fitzgerald's novels. It sprawls awkwardly over some four hundred pages and reads as if Fitzgerald, with his lifelong admiration of the sturdy courage with which Theodore Dreiser had handled his socially important themes, was determined to imitate Dreiser's notorious faults of form as well. The verbally hypersensitive Fitzgerald could never compose the kind of journalistic jargon that is the hallmark of Dreiser's prose. But he does make an attempt to create, instead of a logical and dramatic construction designed to turn the raw material of life into consummate art, a ponderous case history which seems to aim at factual truth rather than at aesthetic beauty and to prove that the two are mercilessly at odds with each other.

In a letter to Thomas Wolfe much later in his life, Fitzgerald was to recommend the attractions of what he called "the novel of selected incidents," setting before the younger writer the kind of carving of which Flaubert was capable in his fiction as opposed to the grubby naturalism of Zola. In his second novel, though, we have an example, if not of full-blown Zolaesque or Dreiserian naturalism, of something apparently inspired by their example. The theme of *The Beautiful and Damned* is failure, but with unintentional appropriateness, it is also a failure as a literary experiment. Fitzgerald had not yet learned precisely how to exploit fully his own strength. After the popular triumph of his first novel, he was apparently attempting to impress the literary world with the fact that he was a "serious" writer and his way of doing this was to write a novel showing as little respect for purity of aesthetic form as the most serious writer in America—Dreiser—habitually did.

Since the characters in Fitzgerald's stories are sometimes given names that point to their destiny (for example, Dick Diver in *Tender Is the Night* plunges from a high station in society to an obscure one), it may be in order to inquire if the hero's name, Anthony Patch (in *The Beautiful and Damned*), is intended to say something about his nature. Fitzgerald says explicitly that the first and middle names of his hero are significant of the moralistic-meddlesome concerns of his grandfather for his full name (of which the middle name was discreetly dropped when he came to be self-conscious about it) is Anthony *Comstock* Patch. The name plainly speaks of the author's satiric intention. And what of the name *Patch* itself, which is punned on at least once in the course of the novel? It is intended, obviously, to point to the "patchy" nature of Anthony's character.

This character, with its lights and shades, seems to lie wholly in the shadow of his grandfather and his civilization. Fitzgerald calls him "one of those personalities who, in spite of all their words, are inarticulate (and) seemed to have inherited only the vast tradition of human failure—that, and the sense of death." Anthony's failure, however, does not disqualify him from being a hero of sorts in Fitzgerald's estimation and perhaps in the estimation of the reader. To Fitzgerald, we must remember, the very imperfections and disadvantages under which a human being labors, may in the long run turn out to be among his most lasting assets.

Anthony Patch is gifted with "the authority of failure" much more generously than was his creator. Anthony does very little if anything in the story except wait for his inheritance and, after endless troubles and litigation which leave him only a shadow of himself, he finally succeeds in getting it. But his very detachment from the social order, combined with his native intelligence, make him a shrewd observer and critic of society. When he reads the Harvard Alumni Bulletin and gets an over-all view of what the members of his class have been doing with their lives, his reflections upon their successes and failures imply the moral standard by which he measures them:

Most of them were in business, it was true, and several were converting the heathen of China or America to a nebulous Protestantism; but a few, he found, were working constructively at jobs that were neither sinecures nor routines. There was Calvin Boyd, for instance, who, though barely out of medical school, had discovered a new treatment of typhus, had shipped abroad and was mitigating some of the civilization that the Great Powers had brought to Servia; there was Eugene Bronson, whose articles in The New Democracy were stamping him as a man with ideas transcending both vulgar timeliness and popular hysteria; there was a man named Daly who had been suspended from the faculty of a righteous university, for preaching Marxian doctrine in the classroom: in art, science, politics, he saw the authentic personalities of his time emerging—there was even Severance, the quarter-back, who had given up his life rather neatly and gracefully with the Foreign Legion on the Aisne.

All this is rather meager as social comment certainly. It seems to be a little on the boyish level of playful rebelliousness against convention and constituted authority that characterizes the concluding pages of *This Side of Paradise*. There are, however, more palpable hits against the current social order in the book. Fitzgerald catches the feverish atmosphere of the stock market speculation that marked the decade of the Twenties, and though he has no impressive ideas of his own to put in the place of the contemporary American notion of what constitutes success, he effectively demolishes this notion with his ridicule. At one point, Anthony, in spite of the "great expectations" which form the leading motive of his uninteresting existence, actually consents to go to work for a firm on Wall Street. Describing that experience, he gives us a representative sampling of American psychology during the boom period:

> During the preceding year, one of the assistant secretaries had invested all his savings in Bethlehem Steel. The story of his spectacular magnificence, of his haughty resignation in January, and of the triumphal palace he was now building in California was the favorite office subject. The man's very name had acquired a magic significance, symbolizing as he did the aspirations of all good Americans. . . . Such was the stuff of life—a dizzy triumph dazzling the eyes of all of them, a gypsy siren to content them with meagre wages and with the arithmetical improbability of the eventual success. . . . Anthony felt that to succeed here the idea of success must grasp and limit his mind. It seemed to him that the essential element in these men at the top was their faith that their affairs were the very core of life. All other things being equal, self-assurance and opportunism won out over technical knowledge; it was obvious that the more expert work went on near the bottom—so, with appropriate efficiency, the technical experts were kept down.

The feeling about technical experts being "kept down" by society is present in all of Fitzgerald's work (he sympathized with the situation of the cameraman in Hollywood, for example, and seems to have thought of himself as belonging to the same category somehow—a kind of master technician with words) but, later on, in the years in which he was at work on *The Last Tycoon,* he came to see the point of view of the entrepreneur, the organizer who was able to put together the separate efforts of many specialists and experts into a larger whole.

In at least one passage, he jabs at a favorite target—what he was to call in *Tender Is the Night*: "the American Woman (whose) clean sweeping irrational temper . . . had broken the moral back of a race and made a nursery out of a continent." In *The Beautiful and Damned,* he calls America

> the most opulent, most gorgeous land on earth—a land whose wisest are but little wiser than its dullest; a land where the rulers have minds like little children and the law-givers believe in Santa Claus; where ugly women control strong men. . . . Yes, it is truly a melancholy spectacle. Women with receding chins and shapeless noses go about in broad daylight saying "Do this!" and "Do that!" and all the men, even those of great wealth, obey implicitly their women to whom they refer sonorously either as "Mrs. So-and-so" or as "The wife."

Gloria Patch, in this second of Fitzgerald's novels, is one of his most interesting feminine creations. Like all of the novelist's heroines, she is beautiful and, like so many of his girls, there is a corrosive cynicism in her verbal expression which is merely the outward form that her profound nihilism takes. Her husband Anthony seems to be speaking for both of them (and for many others in their prematurely life-weary generation) when he says to his friend Maury Noble: "It being a meaningless world, why write? The very attempt to give it purpose is purposeless." In such a directionless universe, the logical credo, quite obviously, is that of Gloria when she denies the existence of any moral standards whatever: "I don't know anything about what you should do or what anybody should do." As Amory Blaine had said in *This Side of Paradise*: "Very few things matter and nothing matters very much." Gloria coins epigrams like some belated follower of George Moore or Oscar Wilde: "There's only one lesson to be learned from life and that is that there's no lesson to be learned from life."

The whole truth about her incurably narcissistic personality is clearly divulged in a speech which she makes while lying ill with double pneumonia and raving feverishly. *In delirium veritas*—the depths of her subconscious are revealed by her wild and whirling words:

Millions of people, swarming like rats, chattering like apes, smelling like all hell . . . monkeys! Or lice, I suppose. For one really exquisite palace . . . on Long Island, say—or even in Greenwich . . . for one palace full of pictures from the Old World and exquisite things—with avenues of trees and green lawns and a view of the blue sea, and lovely people about in slick dresses . . . I'd sacrifice a hundred thousand of them, a million of them . . . I care nothing for them—understand me?

Gloria manages to be even more antisocial than Anthony, who is critical of her: "What he chiefly missed in her mind was the pedantic teleology—the sense of order and accuracy, the sense of life as a mysteriously correlated piece of mechanism." As for Anthony himself, the sense of order that he possesses appears to be minimal and his "philosophy" is as pessimistic in its orientation as that of the philosopher Schopenhauer, to whom he seems indebted for some of his formulations of his feeling: "Desire just cheats you. It's like a sunbeam skipping here and there about a room. It stops and gilds some inconsequential object, and we poor fools try to grasp it—but when we do, the sunbeam moves on to something else, and you've got the inconsequential part, but the glitter that made you want it is gone."

Connected with this pessimism, this almost complete despair of the possibility of more than ephemeral satisfactions in existence, is Fitzgerald's disgusting picture of old age in his account of Adam J. Patch, Anthony's father. The only comparable example in modern literature is that passage in Proust's last volume *Le temps retrouvé*, in which the narrator describes so poignantly and satirically the changes wrought by age in the physiognomies, manners, and even the spirit of his contemporaries. Fitzgerald says of old Adam J. Patch:

The span of his seventy-five years had acted as a magic bellows—the first quarter century had blown him full with life, and the last had sucked it all back. It had sucked in the cheeks and the chest and the girth of arm and leg. It had tyrannously demanded his teeth, one by one, tweaked out his hairs, changed him from gray to white in some places, from pink to yellow in others, callously transposing his colors like a child trying over a paintbox. Then through his body and his soul it had attacked his brain. It had sent him night-sweats and tears and unfounded dreads. It had split his intense normality into credulity and suspicion.

One of the cruelest ironies of the social order stressed by Fitzgerald is that the same man who has seventy-five "winters on his head" also possesses, thanks to the $75,000,000 he has accumulated, privileges and prestige enjoyed by few others among us. He alone, who has lost all taste for living, retains the motives that make life worthwhile: "This feeble, unintelligent old man was possessed of such power that, yellow journals to the contrary, the men in the republic whose souls he could not have bought directly or indirectly would scarcely have populated White Plains. . . ." In *The Beautiful and Damned*, we have the tragic spectacle of youth, which ought to be an end in itself, compelled by social exigencies to spend much of its time plotting and planning to lay hold of the old man's $75,000,000. By the time Anthony and Gloria have succeeded in reaching their ignoble objective, anything in them that even faintly promised to make them worthwhile people is hopelessly lost. Instead of the gay and attractive creatures they had first impressed the world as being, they are as hideous and disfigured as the penurious old capitalist whose will they have spent their lives fighting and have succeeded in breaking at last in death.

In Fitzgerald's writings, the pathos of age and the sense of reverence due to the aged is constantly overweighed by a realization of its unaesthetic qualities. These qualities are illustrated not only in the unflattering portrait of Adam J. Patch but in the one (produced in the same period) of the hero's father in Fitzgerald's only play, *The Vegetable*. Jerry Frost's old father "Dada" in that play is described as having "faded, vacant eyes. . . . Half the time his mind is a vacuum, in which confused clots of information and misinformation drift and stir—the rest of the time he broods upon the minute details of his daily existence."

The fact that the characters a novelist creates bear a resemblance to each other was never more true than of Fitzgerald's women. The mayhem which the author performs upon Gloria Patch is so similar to that done upon Rosalind, the debutante in *This Side of Paradise*, upon Daisy Buchanan in *The Great Gatsby*, upon Nichole Diver in *Tender Is the Night*, and upon numerous girls in his shorter stories that the subject deserves at least brief discussion.

In the short story "The Adjuster," Luella Hemple, who says to a woman companion: "Even my baby bores me." is a variation upon Daisy Buchanan in her habitual mood when she says: "What shall we do with ourselves this afternoon, and the day after that, and the next thirty years?" (The ennui and purposelessness of this are echoed in Eliot's "Waste Land" which Fitzgerald admired very much. "What shall we do tomorrow?/ What shall we ever do?" and also in Auden's line: "What does it mean? What are we going to do?")

In "The Adjuster," Fitzgerald makes a generalization which, no doubt, illuminates his life and work: "It is one of the many flaws in the scheme of human relationships that selfishness in women has an irresistible appeal to many men." The basic common denominator of most of the women in Fitzgerald's stories is their intense self-centeredness. The best example of this other than Gloria Patch is probably Daisy Buchanan, and Daisy's most symbolic action is caught by Fitzgerald in his sentence: "Daisy took her face in her hands as if feeling its lovely shape. . . ."

In the story "May Day," Edith's attitude to Gordon Sterrett is essentially like that of Daisy to Gatsby. Like Daisy, Edith is morally weak and abandons her interest in her lover as soon as she realizes that he is in real trouble. She simply gets scared and runs out on him. In the story "A Short Trip Home" (from *Taps at Reveille*) the character Ellen reminds the reader both of Daisy and of Edith. Like them, she abandons Joe Jelke when the latter is hit by a "hard-looking customer" with brass knuckles. " 'It was Joe's own fault,' she said surprisingly, 'I told him not to interfere.' This wasn't true. She had said nothing, only uttered one curious little click of impatience."

In *The Vegetable,* the wife of the hero, Charlotte Frost, is described in the following terms:

> She's thirty, and old for her age, just like I told you, shapeless, slack-cheeked but still defiant. She would fiercely resent the statement that her attractions have declined ninety per cent since her marriage, and in the same breath she would assume that there was a responsibility and shoulder it on her husband. She talks in a pessimistic whine and, with a sort of dowdy egotism, considers herself generally in the right. Frankly I don't like her, though she can't help being what she is.

The American Woman, then, as she emerges from Fitzgerald's pages, is a badly battered ideal. If he had ever managed to finish his projected novel, "The Boy Who Killed His Mother" one may surmise that the hero's action would have appeared wholly understandable. *This Side of Paradise* had opened with the sentence: "Amory Blaine inherited from his mother every trait except the stray inexpressible few that made him worthwhile." These words begin the procession of phenomenally unappealing females (in the moral rather than the physical sense) that were destined to populate his books.

Yet Van Wyck Brooks could ask with seeming justification in *The Opinions of Oliver Allston*: "Who had ever been more romantic than Scott Fitzgerald?" As with other romantics, however, the letdown was directly proportional to the extreme illusion which had preceded it. In this respect, Fitzgerald has something in common with both Schopenhauer and Proust. His disillusion, like theirs, goes so far that he calls the value of life itself into question. Like them, too, he seems to have become something of a misogynist. He is, of course, not quite so outspoken as Schopenhauer in his contempt for "the narrow-shouldered, broad-hipped, short-legged, unaesthetic sex," nor is he a dissembler of his real feelings like Proust, who worshiped the embalmed memory of his mother's goodness while acting as a sexual deviate who could not form satisfactory relations with other members of her sex. Fitzgerald at first glance appears to be much more conventional than either of these writers, but when the surface is critically penetrated and his conformity to heterosexual mores is dissolved by analysis, he appears to exhibit quite as much anger as any writer has at what he regards as the betrayal of his capacity for love by unresponsive, narcissistic, designing women.

3

THE GREAT GATSBY

I F CRITICAL AND POPULAR OPINION are to be taken as the criteria, *The Great Gatsby* is one of the few important works to come out of contemporary American literature. Moreover, Fitzgerald's third novel is a work of art which, like good wine, seems to get better with age. John Dos Passos has said in his note on Fitzgerald: "It's the quality of detaching itself from its period that marks a piece of work as good." Judged by this rigorous standard, *The Great Gatsby* is very good indeed.

Reading it over again is both easy and pleasant, because it is one of the most compressed and concise of the great novels in any language. It can be compared in this respect to Turgenev's masterpiece *Fathers and Sons,* with which Fitzgerald's book has much in common. Aside from similarity of length, they are both representative of a whole civilization at a critical point in its history.

But the more one looks at the work both as a whole and as a collection of separable elements, the less it seems possible to account for its tremendous effect or to explain the inner mechanism by which this effect is secured.

T. S. Eliot, who read *Gatsby* three times, was never able to send Fitzgerald the promised analysis to support the observation made in his letter that "this remarkable book . . . seems to me to be the first step that American fiction has taken since Henry James . . . . When I have the time, I should like to write to you more fully and tell you exactly why."

The sheer efficiency with which this little novel works upon the mind of the reader gives rise to the increasing respect it inspires. Within its strict confines, the writer has succeeded in capturing and giving form to his impressions of a vast and chaotic world. One is surprised at this realization, as one is surprised that some ladies' wrist watches, despite their phenomenally compact size, should accurately tell time. No American prose work of the twentieth century better exemplifies the epigram from the Greek Anthology: "Out of the jewel, grass is grown." Out of the two hundred pages of

Gatsby spring the turbulent 1920s in America with the same live-liness and spontaneity with which Proust's rural Combray sprang out of his cup of tea.

In rereading the book, we become aware that there are certain words which seem to be repeated over and over again with the insistency of a leitmotiv—words like "lurch," "riotous," "glitter," "romantic." A recurrent symbol, like that of the mysterious eyes of Dr. T. J. Eckleburg, an oculist's abandoned advertising sign hover-ing critically over the wasteland where much of the action takes place, also serves to bind together the varied dramatic materials of the book. Words, phrases, and symbols are not chosen haphazardly; none is used merely for its own sake; all contribute to the profound feeling of unity which makes the book greater than the sum of its separate parts.

Consider, for instance, the aptness of the word "lurches" in a passage describing the first of Gatsby's garden parties: "The lights grow brighter as the earth *lurches* away from the sun, and now the orchestra is playing yellow cocktail music, and the opera of voices pitches a key higher." The unexpected verb "lurches" applied to the noun earth strongly suggests that the world Fitzgerald is de-scribing is on a binge. The concentration of implications achieved in the imagery of the entire sentence is reminiscent of the effects one finds in the best romantic poetry, as, for example, in the line from Keats's "Nightingale": "O for a beaker full of the warm South."

The verb "lurches" is used once again, though less startlingly, in connection with the movement of Gatsby's automobile: "One morn-ing late in July, Gatsby's gorgeous car *lurched* up the rocky drive to my door. . . ." In close alliance to the suggestion in the word "lurches" is the word "riot," which appears over and over again in various connections in the book. On one of the opening pages, the locale of the story is identified as "that slender *riotous* island which extends itself due east of New York." That Gatsby should gravitate there is understandable; it is the attraction of like for like. Describ-ing the earlier years of his hero, the narrator says of him that "his heart was in a constant, turbulent riot." When the narrator wishes to put in a "conscientious" hour at the Yale Club studying invest-ments and securities, he is disturbed by the fact that "there were generally a few rioters around."

"Glitter" in the sense of something that is at the same time both attractive and meretricious is used not only in *Gatsby* but in many of Fitzgerald's stories and novels. It is his favorite word, and he fully exploits its ambiguity of associations. But it is the word "romantic" that appears with the greatest frequency in this particular novel. It is used in all sorts of connections both by the narrator and by the other characters. The mystery surrounding the antecedents of Gatsby, we are told, inspires "romantic speculation" among his guests. The midwestern narrator, Nick, gets to like New York after a while—to like to walk up Fifth Avenue at night "and pick out romantic women from the crowd and imagine that in a few minutes I was going to enter their lives, and no one would ever know or disapprove." In another scene, the very sunshine seems to fall "with romantic affection" upon Daisy's glowing face. Daisy herself uses the word in an ironic tone to her husband Tom, when she is tormented by the knowledge that he has taken up with a new mistress. She says to her dinner guests: "There's a bird on the lawn that I think must be a nightingale come over on the Cunard or White Star Line. He's singing away. . . . It's romantic, isn't it, Tom?" And Tom, whose dinner has just been spoiled by the interruptions of telephone calls from the pertinacious Mrs. Wilson, replies miserably, "Very romantic." When Jordan Baker describes the beginning of the affair between Daisy and Gatsby in Louisville, she uses the words: "Because it seemed romantic to me I have remembered the incident ever since." And when Daisy attends one of Gatsby's fabulous parties, the narrator remarks, "After all, in the very casualness of Gatsby's party there were romantic possibilities totally absent from her world."

Of course, the author himself (in contrast with his characters) is not taken in by these romantic elements. He handles them with the same rubber gloves and antiseptic irony with which Flaubert had "disinfected" the romantic material of *Madame Bovary*. Fitzgerald's formula is to mix in a dash of romance with a liberal portion of the most brutal realism and then to drench the whole thing in irony. The combination is exemplified in a description of a Hollywood actress in *The Last Tycoon*: "Stahr stopped beside her chair. She wore a low gown which displayed the bright eczema of her chest and back. Before each take, the blemished surface was plastered over with an emollient, which was removed immediately after the take. Her hair was of the color and viscosity of drying blood, but there was starlight that actually photographed in her eyes." Indeed, the world of Fitzgerald, like the skin of this actress, is covered with a bright eczema and plastered over with a camouflaging emollient.

The calculated repetitions of words like "lurch," "riot," "glitter," and "romantic" are motivated by the demands of design and composition. "The novel of selected incidents" which Fitzgerald set up before Thomas Wolfe as the model of fiction is compressed into a small space because it is so cunningly wrought. There is little if any improvisation in it. It is a construction, a machine made of words cleverly mimicking the grace of the purely organic world. The fact that everything in it is meticulously planned is evident from the manuscripts of the many drafts which Fitzgerald made of almost every scene in his novels. It is evident also from the adroit way in which the mysteriously symbolic "eyes of Dr. T. J. Eckleburg" (one of the most original inventions in *Gatsby,* which was inspired by a sketch for its dust-jacket when it was ready for publication) were incorporated into the story and alluded to rhythmically at various strategic points until they became wholly characteristic and indispensable elements of it.

Fitzgerald aimed to let the little that remained after innumerable siftings and revisions do the work of everything that had been left out. To do this most effectively, it was necessary not only to choose the precise word (in the Flaubertian sense) but also to find the only space into which it might be fitted. Two centuries before, Jonathan Swift defined excellence of style as "proper words in proper places." The style of Fitzgerald at its best seems to match the requirements of this definition. There is not a wasted motion or breath. Fitzgerald, in one of his notes for the unfinished *Tycoon,* sums up both his aim and accomplishment when he writes: "The impression must be conveyed, but be careful to convey it once and not rub it in. If the reader misses it, let it go—don't repeat."

Fitzgerald is able to communicate impressions of character in his descriptions of posture, tone of voice, and fleeting movements. For example, long before the narrator discovers that Jordan Baker is an incurable liar who has been involved in some golf scandal, he perceives that "her chin (is) raised a little, as if she were balancing something on it which was quite likely to fall." He makes us aware of the significance of her "erect carriage, which she accentuated by throwing her body forward like a young cadet." The characterization brings to mind that of the very minor character in Proust, Madame de Gallardon. The outlines of both personalities are apparently similar (Madame de Gallardon is described as "a scandalous old woman" even as Jordan Baker is a scandalous young woman). Proust's characterization, in this instance, leans far in the direction of caricature, but the basic import that he is seeking to convey is the same as that evidently intended by Fitzgerald. Madame de Gallardon, says Proust, "flung her shoulders proudly back until they seemed to part company with her bust." And a little later on he adds: "Successive mortifications had given her a backward tilt, such as one may observe in trees which have taken root on the very edge of a precipice and are forced to grow backward to preserve their balance."

Both Fitzgerald and Proust observed the connection between unstable character in women (continually hovering on the very edge of an abyss of disgrace were they to be found out) and, as the latter observed, a meretricious "sort of 'bearing' which was accepted by the plebeian as a sign of breeding, and even kindled, at times, a momentary spark in the jaded eyes of old gentlemen in clubs."

The helpless, stumbling, intellectual barrenness of Tom Buchanan is conveyed in his confusions—of names (as when he recalls the name Stoddard—author of *The Rise of the Colored Empires,* who is mentioned again later in the book, because his work is in Gatsby's library—in the form of "Goddard") and of facts—he says: "I read somewhere that the sun's getting hotter every year. It seems that pretty soon the earth's going to fall into the sun—or wait a minute— it's just the opposite—the sun's getting colder every year." He produces a hilarious malapropism when he informs us that he wishes to attend one of Gatsby's parties "in oblivion" meaning presumably *incognito.*

Side by side with this aspect of Tom's character is another element deriving from his physical prowess and manifesting itself in his penchant for pushing people around. In one of the first sentences we read about him, he is "turning [the narrator] around by one arm" to show him the extent of his grounds, which he has acquired from "Demaine, the oil man." Almost immediately thereafter (in spite of Fitzgerald's lightness of touch in these matters) he has Tom turning the narrator Nick "around again, politely and abruptly." And the characteristic appears again and again, most imaginatively rendered: "Wedging his tense arm imperatively under mine, Tom Buchanan compelled me from the room as though he were moving a checker to another square." And some pages later, "I went up to New York with Tom on the train one afternoon and when we stopped by the ashheaps he jumped to his feet and, taking hold of my elbow, literally forced me from the car."

It is characteristic of Tom, too, that he is forever interrupting people's conversations—his wife's, Jordan's. When his imperious will is crossed by his mistress, Mrs. Wilson, he responds immediately by breaking her nose ("making a short, deft movement . . . with his open hand"). In every word and deed, Tom Buchanan, the multi-millionaire who travels around the country with a string of polo ponies, reveals himself to be as completely common, mean, and vulgar as Proust's Duke of Guermantes. The resemblance between these two gentlemen of leisure extends to the countless infidelities with which each of them brutally harasses his charming wife.

Nick Carraway, the narrator of *Gatsby,* is one of Fitzgerald's happier inventions. It is he who sets the moral tone of the story. He gives to it its unity and meaning. In a time gone completely astray on the question of ethical standards, he represents the bulwark of the ethical life. He, at least, in the last analysis, has not lost sight of the old-fashioned landmarks of a religious past; he has retained his belief in the continued validity of the criteria furnished by religion in a nihilistic age. But Fitzgerald, who was wary of his own tendency (as he put it) to preach to people, has by no means simply identified himself (or expected such identification from his readers) with the narrator's viewpoint. For, along with undeniably admirable characteristics, there is in Nick Carraway something priggish and excessively conscious of social convention. Is he not, at least at times, suggestive of a whited sepulchre as well? His virtue stands out not so much by itself as by the contrast which exists between even its tarnished brilliance and the unrelieved blackness all around him in the world. That Nick is a prig, who is simply a snob on the question of his own moral superiority, is clearly indicated on the very first page of the book when he complacently quotes the advice given to him by his father: "Whenever you feel like criticizing anyone, just remember that all the people in the world haven't had the advantages that you've had." The interpretation which the son puts upon this observation is a far-reaching one—it is no less than that "a sense of the fundamental decencies is parcelled out unequally at birth."

It is, of course, disarming that Nick calls himself a snob, but Fitzgerald really did make him a snob, a self-righteous Puritan who boasts of such things as having been drunk only twice in his life, and whose instinctive reaction when he learns of Tom's infidelity to Daisy is, as he puts it, "to telephone immediately for the police." There is a sophisticated irony in his tone when he adds: "It seemed to me that the thing for Daisy to do was to rush out of the house, child in arms" (which sounds almost like an echo of

Eliot's "Waste Land"—a favorite poem of Fitzgerald's—"I shall rush out as I am, and walk the streets/ With my hair down, so."). Yet in spite of the self-mockery in the tone of this expression, Nick means what he says, and the melodramatic sentiment is justified by the series of melodramatic events which are chronicled in the story. Carraway confesses to a desire to know Tom's mistress, but he does not wish to be formally introduced to her ("Though I was curious to see her, I had no desire to meet her . . ."). His relation to Jordan Baker has something of the same duplicity. He is simultaneously attracted and repelled by her, and the revelation of her dishonesty does not mark the end of their affair, as it might have done if Nick were as integral, single minded, and straightforward as he likes to think himself. Some last barrier of moral strength exists in Nick nevertheless. This barrier is the source of much of the particular quality of the book. His strength is shown by his confession that he is "slow-thinking and full of interior rules that act as brakes on my desires." In other words, he possesses that kind of "inner check" of which both Emerson and Irving Babbitt have spoken and which is characteristic of the New England moralist at his best.

Fitzgerald's problem was to make his fictitious alter ego just corrupt enough to be attracted by corruption (and therefore in a position to tell the story) and yet to have him retain that last residue of moral decency which would hold him back somehow at the very brink of the abyss to which curiosity and the casual tides of contemporary indifference had brought him. But there is, apart from his moral quality, a certain superiority which separates him from the other characters. Compared with him intellectually, they are afflicted not merely with blind spots—they actually are blind to a whole dimension of human experience. He sees life in depth as they do not; he sees it objectively as they do not; and he is mature as they are not. When, toward the end of the story, he feels, in talking to Tom Buchanan, "as though I were talking to a child," he is not boasting, for, because of intellectual advantages as well as moral ones, he has grown up as Tom never has and never will.

When Nick, describing the "love-nest" of Tom and Myrtle Wilson, suddenly imagines how their line of yellow-lit windows must appear to the eyes of "the casual watcher in the darkening streets" he adds this striking observation: "And I was him too, looking up and wondering. I was within and without, simultaneously enchanted and repelled by the inexhaustible variety of life." In saying this, he recalls the speaker of Whitman's *Song of Myself* when the latter says in words suggestive of Fitzgerald's: "Apart from the pulling and hauling stands what I am/ Both in and out of the game and watching and wondering at it." It is the ability to feel oneself simultaneously "both in and out of the game," "within and without," that is the true qualification of the objective observer of the human scene. Those not inside the scene they attempt to describe should suffer from a lack of compassionate understanding, yet those too deeply "in" might become sloppy, sentimental, inaccurate—in a word, self-centered. "Cast a cold eye," advised Yeats, but those requisitely cold and nothing more are as false to their trust as those without any coldness, distance, or objectivity at all. Fitzgerald's narrator and Whitman's announcer are gifted with just the right admixture of sympathy and objectivity.

The character who gives the book its title is, as one would expect, more complex and enigmatic than any other. In some ways, he is made to resemble a character of Conrad whom Fitzgerald admired: Lord Jim. He is an actor in every respect, even down to his change of name—from the prosaic James Gatz to the "poetic" Jay Gatsby. At seventeen he makes up the costume which he is to wear for the rest of his life: "So he invented just the sort of Jay Gatsby that a seventeen-year-old boy would be likely to invent, and to this conception he was faithful to the end."

There is some evidence for believing that in making Gatsby resemble an actor who regarded life itself as his stage, Fitzgerald thought that he was drawing a universal human characteristic—as Shakespeare did when he called life a stage and all men and women players. If Fitzgerald's view differs from that of Shakespeare at all, it is only in thinking that the individual human being, far from playing many parts in his time, is really stuck with one part only— a part created by his adolescent imagination and traumatically adhered to in his later life even when it proves anything but appropriate. Tom Buchanan, for example, was bound to "drift on forever seeking, a little wistfully, for the dramatic turbulence of some irrecoverable football game."

It is characteristic of Gatsby that he has virtually no language of his own. His monotonously iterated expression, "old sport," which is redolent of the 1890s rather than of the 1920s, is symbolic of his lack of words. Like his richer rival Tom Buchanan, he is a newcomer to the realm of ideas. He has many more books in his library than he has read; most of them, in fact, are for show and the intellectual "Owl-eyes" discovers that their pages are uncut. Gatsby has evidently been impressed in the same way Tom has by the racist theories of Stoddard (recommended during this period by an editorial in *The Saturday Evening Post*), which represent just the kind of half-baked intellectualism that would impress the cultural parvenu.

In fact, he may be said to communicate most powerfully, as Hemingway's heroes were to do a little later on, not so much by what he says as by his *silences!* He is perhaps the first in the line of strong, silent men who were to people American fiction in the following years. He is, in this respect, entirely unlike heroes such as Hamlet, Faust, or Raskolnikov, who all talk to excess, because they feel compelled (in Hamlet's words) "like a whore" to unpack their hearts with words. For words to be effective there must be behind them both mind and some commonly recognized and accepted standard of values. Men like Gatsby or Jake Barnes in *The Sun Also Rises* make small claim to the possession of mind and they live in a world in which all standards are disintegrating.

The narrator, Nick, is surprised to find that a man who arouses so much interest and speculation among his guests is intellectually as barren and uninteresting as Gatsby: "I had talked with him perhaps six times in the past month and found, to my disappointment, that he had little to say." But such men express themselves not by set speeches, nor even by their actions, but by the sensation of what they are in themselves. Jake Barnes, for instance, is not only silent most of the time but impotent as well. Yet this does not keep him from making himself subtly and strongly felt, almost in the same way an animal might make itself felt in spite of its dumbness. Hemingway excels at communicating precisely the kind of impression that such a nonverbal, morally inactive character might be expected to make. This impression accounts for a great deal of his peculiar effect.

Gatsby in this book is made most vivid to the reader in the same instinctive way. Here is one description of him:

> He was balancing himself on the dashboard of his car with that resourcefulness of movement that is so peculiarly American—that comes, I suppose, with the absence of lifting work or rigid sitting in youth and, even more, with the formless grace of our nervous, sporadic games. This quality was continually breaking through his punctilious manner in the shape of restlessness. He was never quite

still; there was always a tapping foot somewhere or the impatient opening and closing of a hand.

The impression of physical grace in Gatsby is like that created by Proust in the case of the Marquis de Saint-Loup. Proust shows Saint-Loup in the act of vaulting gracefully across the back of a bench in a restaurant in order to reach his seat without disturbing those already seated before him. The carefree movement of Saint-Loup, the soldier and aristocrat, is identified by Proust as the outward sign of his thorough breeding. And Gatsby, too, is a thoroughbred, though of another order. He is the ordinary American, the natural aristocrat, the incarnation of the romantic dream of the noble savage. He is Whitman's common man, who never knew how it felt to stand in the presence of superiors or to take off his hat to any man or to any number of men. We need not be surprised, since he is so representative of a whole class of men to be found in our country in an abundance never before matched, to have this natural aristocrat also described by Fitzgerald as "an elegant young roughneck!"

The character of Gatsby leads naturally into an inquiry about the theme of the book as a whole. This theme seems to have something in common with that of a book published in the same year as *The Great Gatsby,* Theodore Dreiser's *An American Tragedy.* If Gatsby could be described fairly as "an elegant young roughneck," Clyde Griffith is simply a young roughneck, uncouth but with pretensions to elegance. The resemblances of ideas which inspire such works must indicate that, whatever meaning one might care to assign to the expression, certain ideas are somehow "in the air" at a given time. A favorable atmosphere, intellectually speaking, helps in their reception on more than one antenna of literary sensibility.

Although the similarity of theme in these two novels appears to be accidental, there undoubtedly did exist a general, long-lasting sympathy between the two authors, even though the outward forms of their work are in such striking contrast to each other. This is all the more surprising in view of the fact that they belong to different generations as well as to different literary schools. Fitzgerald was twenty-five years younger than Dreiser, yet the evidence for the strange and unexpected affinity of thought and sensitivity between them seems conclusive.

It begins with Fitzgerald's letter of June 3, 1920, to John Grier Hibben, the president of Princeton University. The letter concerns

This Side of Paradise and in it Fitzgerald says: "My view of life, President Hibben, is the view of (the) Theodore Dreisers and Joseph Conrads—that life is too strong and remorseless for the sons of men." In April 1924, we find B. F. Wilson reporting in *Smart Set* a statement by Fitzgerald that "I consider H. L. Mencken and Theodore Dreiser the greatest men living in the country today." Fitzgerald and Dreiser met personally in January 1923 at a celebrated party in Dreiser's apartment and the younger writer presented him with "a really good bottle of Champagne" as a token of his artistic esteem. Concerning the unfinished novel which was to have followed *The Great Gatsby* and which he entitled at various times "The World's Fair," "Our Type," and "The Boy Who Killed His Mother," Fitzgerald wrote to his editor at Scribner's, Maxwell Perkins, on February 8, 1926: "In a certain sense my plot is not unlike Dreiser's in the *American Tragedy*." Indeed the resemblance of the abortive product of his imagination to the work of Dreiser must have attained a certain degree of notoriety, at least among his close friends, for in April 1926 we find Ernest Hemingway writing him a satirical letter in which he pretends that *The Sun Also Rises* is going to have the same plot as "The Boy Who Killed His Mother": "The scene in which Sophia gives birth to twins in the death house at Sing Sing where she is waiting to be electrocuted for the murder of the father and sister of her, as then, unborn children I got from Dreiser." In the magazine *The Bookman* of May 1926, Fitzgerald published a short essay entitled "How To Waste Material: A Note on My Generation" (reprinted in the posthumous *Afternoon of an Author: A Selection of Uncollected Stories and Essays* by Fitzgerald), in which he contrasts Dreiser favorably with Henry James! "For one Dreiser who made a single-minded and irreproachable choice [with reference to that 'question of material' which 'has hampered the American writer' from the beginning] there have been a dozen like Henry James who have stupid-got with worry over the matter. . . ." And on July 7, 1938, a scant two years before his death in Hollywood, we find Fitzgerald compiling a reading list for his daughter at Vassar College and recommending to her attention James's *Daisy Miller* and *Roderick Hudson,* Conrad's *Lord Jim,* and Dreiser's *Sister Carrie* which he describes to her as "damn good . . . almost the first piece of American realism . . . and . . . as easy reading as a True Confession." The enthusiasm for Dreiser's work was evidently both an early and a lasting one.

It is easier to see the differences between Fitzgerald and Dreiser than it is to note their similarities. Their social and cultural backgrounds were as far apart as possible from each other, and the difference between their experiences is reflected in their imaginative constructions. Fitzgerald, if not one of the very rich himself, had ample opportunity to observe and associate with this class at Princeton, New York, Long Island, the Riviera, and Hollywood. At the impressionable age at which Fitzgerald was receiving a fashionable education, Dreiser was being exposed to the vulgar atmosphere of the city-rooms of newspapers, Broadway bars, gambling rooms, and the like. No wonder, then, that Fitzgerald is perfectly at home in portraying fashionable society, while Dreiser is notably weak in depicting the world of the very rich.

Yet each of these storytellers has succeeded in catching a representative image of American life in our time. Clyde Griffiths and Jay Gatsby divide the empire of their country's twentieth-century imagination between them. No characters in first-rate fiction of the period are even remotely as *central* in the aims and ambitions that guide their lives as are these two. Compared to them, Hemingway's Jake Barnes in *The Sun Also Rises* or Popeye in Faulkner's *Sanctuary* are perceived to be hopelessly eccentric with respect to contemporary American civilization. The feeling of what makes for the *centrality* of any given literary image of a society is difficult, perhaps impossible, to define even for those who have an immediate intuition of it in direct experience. It is completely impossible to grasp for those who do not have such experience. This may account for the serious underestimation of both Fitzgerald and Dreiser (as compared with some of their contemporaries) by influential European critics. One must read Fitzgerald in a French version (*Gatsby le magnifique*) to be aware of how much that is characteristic of him disappears from his work in any language but English. The series of minute, incommunicable felicities that distinguish his work in the original is absent from the translation and the hero becomes just another fabulously wealthy gangster of the Prohibition era. All the lyric poetry of the work has wholly disappeared.

The importance of an artist's choice of subject cannot be overestimated. It would be comforting to believe that the artist's superiority could be expressed upon the most indifferent materials. The facts, however, seem to point to another conclusion. John Milton spent a good many years searching for a proper subject upon which to expend his epic powers. Goethe spent some sixty years of his life treating the subject of Faust, which he had come upon early but did not master until very late. Dostoevski spent ten years preparing to write a fictionalized life of Christ but in the end gave up the attempt. The same fate overtook Tolstoi's projected sequel to *War and Peace* which was to have dealt with the Decembrist Revolt of 1825. On the other hand, the subject of *Anna Karenina* imposed itself upon Tolstoi's mind by force and compulsively gripped him until he had completed writing the novel.

It is not accidental that certain subjects appeal for their rendition to specific artists. The artist's power may be constant, yet it is not a matter of indifference as to whether he succeeds in finding just the right subject that will develop his talent to its fullest. The theme of the poor boy in America, who is willing to proceed to any length of lawlessness, even murder, in order to satisfy his own dreams and, perhaps more important, the dreams of the rich girl to whom he is hopelessly enslaved emotionally—such is the common denominator of both *An American Tragedy* and *The Great Gatsby*.

We know something of the genesis of both books in the minds of their authors. In Dreiser's case, as we know from the biographical reminiscences of his second wife Helen, he had long been fascinated by what he regarded as the typical American social crime—the kind which he described in his book. But the story he actually used did not come to him all at once. He collected data on at least fifteen crimes similar in basic form to the one he settled on as his subject. On one of these crimes (the murder of the Hyannis girl Avis Linnell by her preacher-lover Richeson) he made an abortive start of a novel and wrote six chapters of it before changing to a fiction based on the murder of Grace Brown by Chester Gillette, which had taken place in 1911 in the locality later used in the book.

The Herculean effort of Theodore Dreiser—ten years elapsed between the writing of the novel preceding *An American Tragedy* and the *Tragedy* itself—was plainly directed at finding a typical case of a socially motivated murder. We may conjecture that he rejected the suitability of the Linnell-Richeson case for his purposes because the fact that the man was a preacher made the case anything but typical. The term *typical* is not to be understood in the sense of being statistically *usual*. A case of murder is obviously an extreme manifestation of human nature—but it makes a considerable difference whether or not the extreme is recognizably related to the norm of thought and behavior in a given society. One need not suppose that *The Brothers Karamazov* or *Crime and Punishment* represented incidents more numerically probable in Russian society than *An*

American Tragedy did in relation to American society. Yet this
does not prevent any of these great works from being representative
in the higher sense of the word.

Fitzgerald, however, had no such long struggle as Dreiser to find
the subject best fitted to enlist his greatest talents. One of the
original models of Jay Gatsby appears to have been a rich rum-
runner whom the author had met and described to Edmund Wilson,
who in turn used the description in his play *This Room, This Gin,
and These Sandwiches*. The casualness of this origin suggests why
The Great Gatsby may have appeared to as good and sympathetic
a reader as H. L. Mencken to be the dramatization of a mere
anecdote! What an anecdote it is though—one which is capable of
taking on the dimensions of myth in our minds. There is something
consciously Homeric in the note that Fitzgerald strikes at times in
Gatsby: "All the lights were going on in West Egg now; the electric
trains, men-carrying, were plunging home through the rain from
New York." And this is only half-parody. It is clear that Fitzgerald,
not wholly without justification, thought of his subject in this novel,
in spite of its seeming slightness of scope and dimensions, as epical.

And whether he himself thought so or not, he did in fact create
in *Gatsby* a character and fable of mythical proportions and epic
grandeur. Gatsby, the romantic gangster, seems as impressive a sum-
mation of the tendencies of an age as was Turgenev's portrait of
the nineteenth-century nihilist, Bazarov. From different yet equally
traditional premises, Fitzgerald's and Turgenev's heroes have arrived
at equally destructive, materialistic conclusions.

The triumph of Fitzgerald is to make the reader feel the attraction
and force of all those old-fashioned rules of moral behavior of which
his characters are unaware. Nobody believes in living "by the
Book" any longer as the Puritans once did—nobody, that is, but the
gullible garage-man Mr. Wilson. The rest act as if they were convinced, together with the adulteress Mrs. Wilson, that "You can't
live forever; you can't live forever." (These were, she tells us, her
last thoughts before she succumbed to the blandishments of Tom
Buchanan.) The moral law, however, to the truly imaginative writer,
appears to be no whimsical or human construction. It is rather
built into the world of reality around us. It never ceases to function
with the most terrifying accuracy and effectiveness.

Fitzgerald's story has something in it as compelling as a Greek
tragedy. How fatefully appropriate it is, for example, that the car

which strikes down Myrtle Wilson on the highway should be driven by the wife she has injured—Daisy Buchanan! The book as a whole (not simply the narrator Nick, whose vision is limited like that of the rest of us) makes us feel that each person in the world receives in strictest measure exactly what he deserves to get. Tom and Daisy, though superficially they escape from the talons of man-made laws, do not really escape from a higher law. They are sufficiently punished in simply being what they are. The saving grace of Gatsby himself is not wasted, even if only in leaving behind a regret in the mind of the narrator and the reader. There are all sorts of commonplaces for this sort of thing—sayings like the one that virtue is its own reward or that vice constitutes its own punishment. There are, however, no commonplaces in Fitzgerald's novel; no visible or creaking mechanisms. Everything about this masterwork is convincing, natural and seamless.

This is one of the few American novels of our time that seem to make a claim to the lasting attention of the author's fellow countrymen. And for once Fitzgerald, who was inclined to beguile himself as to the real value of his work so long as it was too close to him in time, was perfectly right in the early estimate he formed of it. We find him writing about it to his friend John Peale Bishop in terms that are at the same time ecstatic and completely realistic: "The novel I'm sure of. It's marvelous." "Maybe my book is rotten but I don't think so" and then again: "Write me the opinion you may be pleased to form of my chef d'oeuvre and others' opinion. Please. I think it's great but because it deals with much debauched material, quick deciders . . . may mistake it. . . ."

4

TENDER IS THE NIGHT

THE DECLINE of Fitzgerald's literary powers began somewhere between *The Great Gatsby* and *Tender Is the Night,* published almost a decade later. It is not particularly felt in *All the Sad Young Men,* the volume of stories published the year after *Gatsby,* and containing one of his greatest works, "The Rich Boy." There are reputable critics, it must be said, who have denied that Fitzgerald's abilities ever waned, but the consensus of opinion is that a decline, though not very perceptible, certainly occurred. To define its exact nature and its cause is not easy. George Bernard Shaw once said that for every hundred critics who can tell an artist that something is wrong with his work, there is perhaps one who can make it clear to him what is wrong and why.

The keynote of Mizener's favorable commentary on *Tender Is the Night* is sounded in the statement: "With all its faults, it is Fitzgerald's finest and most serious novel." Further expanding this sentiment, he says: "The book's defects are insignificant compared to its sustained richness of texture, its sureness of language, the depth and penetration of its understanding—not merely of a small class of people, as so many reviewers thought, but of the bases of all human disaster." Mizener suggests the defects of the book when he speaks of its "structure [being] damaged by failure to solve the problem of point of view." But he finds the very excellence of form which is undeniable in *The Great Gatsby* somehow associated with a certain superficiality. He says: "The scope of *Tender Is the Night* is such that, for all the book's faults, its philosophical impact is unforgettable. It makes *The Great Gatsby,* which, in structure so perfectly satisfies 'the cannons' [*sic*] of the dramatic novel, seem neat and simple."

To a reader like Mizener, *Tender Is the Night,* far from being slightly anticlimactic, is the high point of Fitzgerald's creative achievement. His opinion finds some support in a letter that Thomas Wolfe wrote to Fitzgerald in 1937 in which he says: "I still think as I always thought that *Tender Is the Night* had in it the best work you have ever done." But this judgment of a fellow craftsman, who makes no pretense to either critical or self-critical acumen, seems significant only in that Wolfe himself was capable of appreciating content more than form, as Fitzgerald tried gently to tell him.

The sounder judgment is to be found in Edmund Wilson's dedicatory epistle to *The Crack-Up* in which, referring apparently to his friend's two best-known works in metaphorical terms, he calls them:

> Two emeralds, green and lucid, one half-cut,
> One cut consummately—both take their place
> In Letters' most expensive Cartier case.

The consummately cut jewel is obviously *The Great Gatsby,* the half-cut one is *Tender Is the Night.* This criticism establishes the correct distinction between the two works. Only by admitting that *Tender Is the Night* stands below *Gatsby* in aesthetic worth does one establish any basis for discovering both its real merits and its obvious defects.

Fitzgerald worked longer and perhaps harder on *Tender Is the Night* than he did on any of his other works. We know that the novel underwent a number of metamorphoses between the time of its conception in 1925 (the same year which saw the publication of *The Great Gatsby*) and the date of its publication in 1934. He made a number of false starts in the actual writing of it during that time, some of which he pursued to considerable length (just as Dreiser wrote six chapters of his abortive version of *An American Tragedy,* based on the Linnell-Richeson case). By themselves, these facts would not mean much—they might have quite logically preceded the production of his masterpiece. From Helen Dreiser's account in her book *My Life with Dreiser,* we know that Dreiser took as long as Fitzgerald did and made almost as many false starts in the composition of his greatest work.

It is the final result that counts, however. The truth is that *Tender Is the Night* never really jelled in its creator's mind; it emerged as a mass of literary protoplasm containing certain unfinished suggestions of possible forms. The public, mostly because of its author's secure reputation as a storyteller, came to glance at it suspiciously, surmised the shapelessness of its form, and quickly turned its attention elsewhere. Social-minded critics such as Malcolm Cowley have been inclined to blame the comparatively poor reception of this novel upon the historical moment of its appearance—during the great depression. Cowley writes *"Tender* was published in the spring of 1934. . . . It dealt with fashionable life in the 1920s at a time when most readers wanted to forget that they had ever been concerned with frivolities; the new fashion was for novels about destitution and revolt. The book had some friendly and even admiring notices, but most reviewers implied that it belonged to the bad old days before the crash; they dismissed it as having a 'clever and brilliant surface' without being 'wise and mature.' "

Cowley's theory sounds plausible at first but upon reflection it runs against some stubborn facts. If critics in this period were intolerant of Fitzgerald because he dealt with the fashionable life of the 1920s, why is it that critical admiration for Proust, who chronicled the fashionable life of the 1890s in the Parisian Faubourg Saint-Germain, reached its high point (in America, at least) during this time? As a matter of fact, there are some marked resemblances between this particular novel of Fitzgerald's and Proust's work not only in subject matter but in style as well. Why, then, was one accepted and the other rejected? Some explanation other than the supposed vogue of the proletarian novel is evidently needed. Fitzgerald himself did not rationalize his failure. He thought that there was something wrong inside his work rather than outside of it. Or as Cowley puts it:

> Fitzgerald didn't blame the public or the critics. It was one of the conditions of the game he played with life to accept the rules as they were written; if he lost point and set after playing his hardest, that was due to some mistake in strategy to be corrected in the future. He began looking in a puzzled fashion for the mistake in *Tender Is the Night.* There must have been an error in presentation that had kept his readers from grasping the richness and force of his material; for a time he suspected that it might merely be the lack of something that corresponded to stage directions at the beginning of each scene.

Unfortunately, what is wrong with the book is nothing so trivial as that. It is not a matter of mere rearrangement of the material— as Fitzgerald later thought—and his suggested change of the order of various chapters (which was adopted in Cowley's edition of the book in the 1950s) not only fails to improve upon the 1934 version but, on the contrary, weakens it still further. The earlier edition, by beginning in the middle of the story (as Aristotle advises the dramatist to do) instead of with a factual exposition of the hero's background, had a dramatic tension and interest which the later version lacks. Nor is it altogether a matter of inadequate "cutting," as Edmund Wilson apparently thought. An author is unable to "cut consummately" unless he has a clear idea of his aims, and everything points to the conclusion that Fitzgerald was fuzzy about his aims in his last two long works—*Tender Is the Night* and *The Last Tycoon*—just as he had been in his first two long works, *This Side of Paradise* and *The Beautiful and Damned.* Only in *The Great Gatsby* was he absolutely clear in his ethical as well as his aesthetic goal, and this clarity, which accounted for the unparalleled success of that book, he owed to the fact that in this work alone he did not hesitate to cling consistently, in the words of Proust, "to the old standards of honor, to the moral landmarks of a period now dead." Here alone he spoke with a voice and an authority made exceptionally resonant by age-old wisdom. After a quarter of a century, the immediate reaction of some readers to *Tender Is the Night* still seems valid—namely, that there is something not quite "wise and mature" about the work.

This may be what Mizener meant in speaking of the "structure" of the novel being "damaged by failure to solve the problem of point of view," but like Wilson, Cowley, and Fitzgerald himself, he probably intended to confine his criticism to a question of form. The "point of view" of which he speaks refers to one or another of the characters through whose eyes we witness the action. Those who spoke of the novel (in its original version) as "breaking in half" must have had in mind the fact that the earlier part of the story is glimpsed through the eyes of an eighteen-year-old Hollywood starlet, Rosemary, while the same scene later is presented to us from a less callow, more grown-up point of view.

The central infirmity of the structure of *Tender Is the Night,* as well as the central strength of *The Great Gatsby,* was indicated by the implications of a passage in an essay about Wyndham Lewis in *The Yale Review* some years ago by Russell Kirk:

The art of satire, as Lewis argues in *Rude Assignment,* can endure only while the satirist stands firm upon a ground of moral principle, from which he can assail his victims with confidence: satire will be written, and read, and applauded, only when writers and the public acknowledge the existence of abiding moral standards. If no values exist, then follies and crimes are not follies and crimes at all, but merely phenomena of meaningless life; and no one will appreciate satire because no one will believe that the satirist is attacking anything of importance.

Fitzgerald certainly had a satiric impulse but this impulse, except on rare occasions, was based upon nothing more substantial than his own feeling of what constituted good taste. Since he had no firm commitment to a belief in the existence of any permanent standards of moral behavior, he is quite as likely in his satire to rely upon certain snobbish assumptions which he shares with his reader as he is to rely upon something stronger which is independent of them both. The very cornerstone of consistent accomplishment, therefore, is lacking in his satire. "If no values exist, then follies and crimes are not follies and crimes at all, but merely phenomena of meaningless life"—this formulation, quite unintentionally, is reminiscent of Fitzgerald's letter to President Hibben of Princeton University: "My view of life, President Hibben, is the view of the Theodore Dreisers and Joseph Conrads—that life is too strong and remorseless for the sons of men." The assumption here is that the phenomena of life cannot possibly have a moral significance since they are "meaningless." Yet, paradoxically, the impulse to satire remained strong in Fitzgerald, finding expression, for example, in his comparison of Gatsby with Trimalchio, the *nouveau-riche* vulgarian depicted by Petronius in his *Satyricon* (one of Fitzgerald's earlier ideas for a title to his own book was "Trimalchio of West Egg").

At the heart of almost all of Fitzgerald's work, we find, instead of a clear moral idea, a dissonance, or ambiguity requiring resolution, or even an outright contradiction. He knew this and, except in periods when he suffered the inevitable consequences of such contradiction, was rather inclined to glory in it as a sign of intellectual superiority. In *The Crack-Up* he says: "Let me make a general observation—the test of a first-rate intelligence is the ability to hold two opposed ideas in the mind at the same time, and still retain the ability to function." (Dryden may have had the same thought when he wrote: "Great wits to madness sure are near allied/ And thin partitions do their bounds divide.") According to this criterion, Fitzgerald undoubtedly possessed a first-rate intelligence, and even, as Mizener would have us believe, a philosophy. This philosophy may perhaps best be summed up in the couplet from William Blake:

54

"Do what you will, this world's a fiction,/ And made up of contradiction." It may be instructive to reflect on the profound difference between Blake's couplet and a sentence in Irving Babbitt which superficially resembles it; in *Literature and the American College*, Babbitt writes: "The true mark of excellence in a man, as Pascal puts it, is his power to harmonize in himself opposite virtues and to occupy all the space between them."

The test of intelligence may be the power of entertaining a number of ideas simultaneously—that is to say, the ability to mediate between them and to *harmonize* them. Fitzgerald's formulation, however, suggests little more than discord and disorder. A mind functioning on the basis of "opposed ideas" is about as reliable an instrument as an electrical system with crossed wiring on the edge of a short circuit. Fitzgerald might have discovered this sad truth if he discovered anything at all as a result of what he called his "crack-up," but like his other experiences this one too remained largely confined to the realm of feeling and was hardly penetrated by reason. Reason, to a romantic like Fitzgerald, is a weapon wielded by the hands of feeling. It leads one in the direction of rationalization or plausible explanation, but not genuine understanding.

Fitzgerald's own conception of the theme of *Tender Is the Night* is contained in one of the notes to himself quoted in Cowley's introduction: "The novel should do this.—Show a man who is a natural idealist, a spoiled priest, giving in for various causes to the ideas of the haute bourgeoisie, and in his rise to the top of the social world losing his idealism, his talent and turning to drink and dissipation. Background one in which the leisure class is at their truly most brilliant and glamorous." Quite aside from the fact that the description (presumably of Dick Diver) does not describe Dick Diver at all (just as the title *Tender Is the Night* was only an afterthought and has no cogent connection with the material of the novel, though it testifies to Fitzgerald's lifelong admiration for John Keats), this passage from his notebooks indicates the basic contradiction about his subject that afflicted him.

While there was always one part of Fitzgerald that was repelled by the "glitter" of the fashionable world, there was another part that was weakly and helplessly enslaved to it. Since "the leisure class . . . at their truly most brilliant and glamorous" represented an immediate value to him, he could not really be expected to sit in judgment upon anyone who succumbed to its attractions. The result of this ambiguity of attitude had been noted early in Fitzgerald's literary career (that is, before the appearance of *The Great Gatsby*) by the critic Paul Rosenfeld:

> What one does affirm . . . is that the author of *This Side of Paradise* and of the jazzy stories does not sustainedly perceive his girls and men for what they are, and tends to invest them with precisely the glamour with which they in pathetic assurance rather childishly invest themselves. . . . The couple in *The Beautiful and Damned,* charming and comely enough and yet portrayed at length in the horrible effort to perpetuate a state of narcissistic irresponsibility, we are begged to perceive as iridescently wonderful bodies and souls.

The substance of this acute criticism is similar to that found in D. W. Harding's review of *Tender Is the Night*: "There is his sensitiveness (occasionally touching sentimentality) and his awareness of the brutalities in civilized people's behavior, and there is simultaneously his keen appreciation, not entirely ironic, of the superficies of these same people's lives." In other words, he is *taken in* by the illusion he himself created; the illusion which, instead, he should have exposed as worthless. It is impossible to have it both ways at the same time—one cannot treat the same object as being truly precious ore, on the one hand, and as being simply a semblance of the real thing on the other hand. Perhaps Fitzgerald thought this could be done, but if so, his work proves that he was mistaken.

H. L. Mencken wrote in his review of *The Great Gatsby*:

> The thing that chiefly interests the basic Fitzgerald is still the florid show of modern American life—and especially the devil's dance that goes on at the top. . . . What engrosses him is the high carnival of those who have too much money to spend and too much time for the spending of it. Their idiotic pursuit of sensation, their almost incredible stupidity and triviality, their glittering swinishness—these are the things that go into his notebooks. . . . In *The Great Gatsby* he comes near the bottom. Social leader and jailbird, grand lady and kept woman, are here almost indistinguishable. We are in an atmosphere increasingly levantine. . . . To find a parallel for the grossness and debauchery that now reign in New York one must go back to the Constantinople of Basil I.

If this were true of Fitzgerald's work in general, he would be a much greater writer—certainly a more consistent and satisfactory one.

Mencken, however, saw in Fitzgerald more than was actually there (or, at least, something different from what was actually there). Fitzgerald was not nearly so pure and undivided in his satiric aim and intention. The inadequate public response to *Tender Is the Night* may have been, in part, due to the public's awareness of Fitzgerald's confused sense of values, which was reflected in the faults of formal structure (the "splitting in half" of the novel) noted by the critics. Of course, the public has responded to books much worse than this one; it has also at times passed by masterpieces for a whole generation (Melville's *Moby Dick* is one example) but in this particular case both the critics and the public alike seem to have detected a real shortcoming in Fitzgerald's work. The public and its judgments are certainly not sacrosanct or infallible indicators of aesthetic values, but neither are they necessarily wrong, as some intellectuals have come to believe.

Edmund Wilson has written: "His conception of his subject in *Tender Is the Night* had shifted in the course of his writing so that the parts of that fascinating novel do not always quite hang together. . . ." It is, however, not simply a matter of the false starts he made or of the survival of earlier versions in the later one— confusing as this tends to become—but a certain confusion as to standards both at the very heart of the book and in the heart of Fitzgerald himself.

There is no better way to illustrate this confusion than to examine the development of the character of Dick Diver. After a brilliant and promising start as a psychiatrist in Zurich and a later career that made him the cynosure of attention in the most fashionable society of the Mediterranean coast of France, he degenerates, at the end of the story, into an obscure, aimlessly philandering country doctor in the smaller towns of upper New York State. There is every indication that Fitzgerald intended to make his last chapter on Dick's career quietly heart-rending in its understatement. Diver ends, not melodramatically (Fitzgerald's plan for him at one time, it seems, was to have him killed) but in a kind of muted anticlimax. In that sense, his fate is like that of the world described by T. S. Eliot in "The Hollow Men," the world that "ends not with a bang but a whimper." Though Fitzgerald changed the order of chapters in the later version of the novel edited by Cowley, so that there is a different beginning and middle section, he left the original ending untouched. It is fair to assume, then, that at the time the story was written, the ending must have seemed satisfactory to him in fulfilling his intentions of communicating the exact shade of feeling he had about the world.

We read in that last chapter (in art as in life we may have to "look to the end" in order most clearly to grasp its meaning):

> Dick opened an office in Buffalo, but evidently without success. Nicole did not find what the trouble was, but she heard a few months later that he was in a little town named Batavia, New York, practising general medicine, and later that he was in Lockport, doing the same thing. By accident she heard more about his life there than anywhere: that he bicycled a lot, was much admired by the ladies, and always had a big stack of papers on his desk that were known to be an important treatise on some medical subject, almost in process of completion. He was considered to have fine manners and once made a good speech at a public health meeting on the subject of drugs; but he became entangled with a girl who worked in a grocery store, and he was also involved in a lawsuit about some medical question; so he left Lockport. . . . In the last letter she had from him he told her that he was practising in Geneva, New York . . . in the heart of the Finger Lakes section. . . . His latest note was postmarked Hornell, New York, which is some distance from Geneva and a very small town; in any case he is almost certainly in that section of the country, in one town or another.

The reader, under the spell of Fitzgerald's elegiac tone of *sic transit gloria mundi,* is quite likely to be depressed by this mournful ending. It is sad to see even the unsympathetically or unscrupulously ambitious man of the world—a Wolsey or a Sejanus—brought low by fortune from the lofty position to which he has so painstakingly raised himself. How much sadder is it, then, to watch a similar fate overtake as charming a character as Dick Diver, whose fault, if he has one, is more an exaggeration of good nature than any positively bad trait. But once we have recovered from our momentary identification with the author's point of view, which he has imposed upon us by the manner of his narration, we may not think that the quasi-tragedy he has described is so tragic in quality after all.

What elements, in this passage, serve to communicate Fitzgerald's feeling about his subject? Dick Diver is inveigled into some sordid affair with a "girl who works in a grocery store"—and the scene of his activity is transferred from one of the greater centers of the world—Geneva, Switzerland—to that place in upper New York State which has nothing of fame but the same name. Upon what does the evaluation to which we are supposed to attach these facts (and which indeed the author himself seems to attach to them) ultimately depend? Is it not a kind of snobbery very far removed from anything that may be called a commonly agreed-on standard of values?

Dick Diver, we must remember, had been introduced by his creator as one who regarded "the fine quiet of the scholar" as the "nearest of all things to heavenly peace." According to this criterion, Geneva, New York, may be as favorable (even more favorable, because of its very lack of worldly distractions) to creative intellectual activity as any other place. This might be especially true of Diver, who has had ample opportunity to travel and to mingle with the best society before retiring to a more provincial life. Proust's *Jean Santeuil* pictures a writer who wishes for a life as a teacher of philosophy in some small place beyond the edge of the fashionable world so that he may carry on the spiritual activity to which his life is dedicated with the least disturbance. On the other hand, Balzac (like Fitzgerald) seems to have regarded as tragic a fate such as this for any man brilliant enough to illuminate the center of the world (Parisian society in his case). Balzac's attitude, we say, was a worldly one, and Proust's an unworldly one (although he was more "at home" in high society than Balzac), but both authors were consistent with the implications of their central points of view concerning life and its values. Fitzgerald's trouble is that, like so many extreme romantics, he vacillated between two contrary views. He wished to lead the good life from a spiritual point of view in the desert of worldly values where it was quite certain in advance that it could not be led.

In Fitzgerald's work, as we have noted, the names of the characters themselves suggest special meanings. There is something trivial sounding about the very name Dick Diver. It would do, perhaps, for the hero of a boy's book and something of the quality suggested by it has gotten into the novel. He is "boyish" not merely in the sense of being not quite mature. It is difficult to believe in his supposed mastery of the art of medicine; he never seems to be serious or adult enough for such an accomplishment. At one point, we learn that he had become interested in his specialty because he had been following a girl who was attending a psychology lecture. This might be the documentary truth about a character's experience but we can hardly accept it as the dramatic truth about him without his forfeiting his claim to our esteem.

Consider, too, the marriage of Dick to Nicole, which is really the whole story of *Tender Is the Night*. It has happened, of course, that physicians, even highly skilled psychiatrists, have become emotionally involved with their own patients. It has also happened that psychiatrists treating others for mental illness have suffered breakdowns themselves. In fact, we see Dick Diver briefly outlined against the background of a psychiatrist who has suffered a collapse and is a patient in Dick's clinic. But these are exceptional cases, and hardly the proper vehicle for such a commentary on human life and society as we may assume the novelist to be interested in making.

The reader is asked to believe that Nicole's mental trouble stemmed from the fact that her father, Devereux Warren, had had sexual intercourse with her when she was a young girl. But has not Freud himself said that the starting point of his important insight was when he realized that his hysterical patients' stories of having been sexually assaulted by their parents when they were young (which previously he had been inclined to accept as the literal truth) were, without exception, fantasies—important fantasies, to be sure, containing a grain of *symbolic* truth, but basically fantasies nonetheless?

Yet it is precisely a fantastic fact such as this that Fitzgerald expects the reader to believe as the explanation for Nicole's emotional disorder. Such an incestuous relationship as the story assumes for its foundation is no doubt possible. But the question is whether it is sufficiently *probable,* in the Aristotelian sense, to perform adequately its assigned function in the story. This question is not merely pedantic. The assumption is that the author here, as in *The Great Gatsby,* has aimed at the construction of a fable and of characters who are representative rather than characters who are unique, extremely special, or simply eccentric.

If *Tender Is the Night* were a case history not merely of Nicole but of Dick Diver himself, how significant would it be as art? Malcolm Cowley writes in the introduction to his edition of *Tender Is the Night*:

> One fault of the earlier version was its uncertainty of focus. We weren't quite sure in reading it whether the author had intended to write about a whole group of Americans on the Riviera—that is, to make the book a social study with a collective hero—or whether he had intended to write a psychological novel about the glory and decline of Richard Diver as a person. Simply by changing the order of the story and starting with Diver as a young doctor in Zurich, Fitzgerald answered our hesitation. We are certain in reading the

final version that the novel is psychological, that it is about Dick Diver, and that its social meanings are obtained by extension or synecdoche. Dick is the part that stands for the whole. He stands for other Americans on the Riviera, he stands for all the smart men who played too close to the line, he even stands for the age that was ending with the Wall Street crash, but first he stands for himself.

This sounds very much as if Cowley had in mind Fitzgerald's own observation about the relation of the individual to the representative at the beginning of his story "The Rich Boy": "Begin with an individual and before you know it you find that you have created a type; begin with a type, and you find that you have created— nothing." As a generalization, this seems quite impressive but its applicability in the particular case is arguable. Emphasis upon the individual is a two-edged method. It is like the observation concerning solitude made by Thomas Mann in *Death in Venice*: "Solitude gives birth to the original in us, to beauty unfamiliar and perilous—to poetry. But also it gives birth to the opposite: to the perverse, the illicit, the absurd." So it is, too, with the individual. On the one hand, the writer may create a Hamlet, an Ivan Karamazov, or an Oedipus, all of whom are so frighteningly representative of humanity that it must be a rare human being who, understanding them, does not see in them, in some measure, a reflection of himself (or, at least, a facet of himself). On the other hand, too exclusive an emphasis upon individuality may lead the writer to lose himself in blind alleys of the eccentric, the grotesque, or the merely bizarre.

In portraying Dick Diver, Fitzgerald, contrary to his intention, both began and ended with an individual, missing completely the "type" which the individual may have represented. This is not to say that he committed what he himself thought of as the cardinal literary sin—the failure to make his character live or be interesting to the reader. It is possible to agree with Edmund Wilson, who finds *Tender Is the Night* fascinating, without believing that the exercise of such a fascination upon our imagination constitutes the highest possible reach for the artist. The greatest stories may or may not be fascinating but they are sure to be something more—they somehow manage to enter the realm of the mythical, which is the permanent aspect of all particular truths. Even Fitzgerald at his best reaches high above the "fascinating" (Gatsby, like the hero of "The Rich Boy," but unlike Dick Diver, is capable of standing for much more than himself).

61

The story line of *Tender Is the Night* seems confused and split within itself. It does not "always quite hang together" because it has not completely emerged from its matrix of the subjective in the author's mind. It is not related by Fitzgerald to a permanent standard of ethical truth as *Gatsby* is, for instance. Fitzgerald does attempt to do this. Dick Diver's father, we are told, is a retired clergyman whom his son remembered as "struggling in poor parishes." Dick loved his father and accepted him as his moral guide: "Again and again he referred judgment to what his father would probably have thought or done." This sentence reminds us of Nick Carraway and the opening pages of *Gatsby*. But unlike Carraway, the father's ethical views are imperfectly realized in the character of Dick. Fitzgerald refers to Dick's character in his notebooks as "comparatively good." His tone of voice rings most sincerely at the moment when, after his father's death, he exclaims at the cemetery: "Good-bye my father—good-bye, all my fathers." He makes explicit in this statement what seems to have been implicit in his conduct all along: that he has long ago departed from his father's criterion of rectitude. How, otherwise, could he have tolerated the set of people among whom he had lived for so long? There is in him, at most, a nostalgic longing for the simple world of his father's belief, but he also has a deep-lying conviction that such a world has vanished, never to return. Furthermore, Fitzgerald himself has no basis upon which he can correct this notion of the character he has created, for he has become too sympathetic and too involved with Dick's point of view to stand far enough apart to judge him.

In *The Great Gatsby,* Nick Carraway holds the line morally speaking, but, as we have indicated, there is a hint, however faint, of something priggish about him. Fitzgerald, it seems, could not make concrete his feeling for the existence of an ethical realm set securely above the flux of experience except in a character like Carraway, who carried a slight odor of sanctimonious self-righteousness. But in *Tender Is the Night,* all the characters are morally at sea, and no bulwark of belief is left in any of them, not even in Dick Diver. There is no character corresponding to Nick Carraway in this novel, no potent symbol such as "the mysterious eyes of Doctor T. J. Eckleburg" of the earlier novel. Only the sense of carnival in *The Great Gatsby* remains in the later one. Fitzgerald failed in his professed intention of showing us "a natural idealist, a spoiled priest, giving in for various causes to the ideas of the haute bourgeoisie." He failed because he could not muster in himself (and, therefore, could hardly communicate to the reader) the conviction that any alternative standard existed.

He has not even succeeded in fulfilling his secondary aim of making the novel's "background one in which the leisure class is at their truly most brilliant and glamorous." There is little either brilliant or glamorous in Fitzgerald's cast of characters as they play on the shores of the Mediterranean. What Albert Thibaudet once wrote of Proust, somewhat imperceptively, is far more applicable to the characters in *Tender Is the Night*. The critic had spoken of "the ultimate nothingness of the people of [the novelist's] world," "an erotic and mysterious group having little in common with the generality of mankind and for whom consequently the ordinary reader must always feel indifference." This description is not true of Proust, but it is true of Fitzgerald, at least so far as this particular novel is concerned. In *The Great Gatsby,* a similar social group has had a significance wrung out of it by the writer in spite of itself. But in *Tender Is the Night* he has himself succumbed to what he had intended to criticize or condemn.

If Fitzgerald failed to communicate in the story any broadly conceived social or satirical purpose he may have had in mind, he did manage to include in it some telling sideswipes at the shortcomings of American civilization, as he saw them. These strokes are sometimes only peripherally related to the main thread of the plot—they have the effect of being the author's editorial comments rather than springing organically from the dramatic requirements. A striking instance of this can be found in Dick's description of the Psychiatric Congress in Berlin:

> He could imagine it well enough, new pamphlets by Bleuler and the older Forel . . . the paper by the American who cured dementia praecox by pulling out his patient's teeth or cauterizing their tonsils, the half-derisive respect with which the idea would be greeted, for no more reason than that America was such a rich and powerful country. The other delegates from America—red-headed Schwartz with his saint's face and his infinite patience in straddling two worlds, as well as dozens of commercial alienists with hangdog faces, who would be present partly to increase their standing, and hence their reach for the big plums of the criminal practice, partly to master novel sophistries that they would weave into their stock-in-trade, to the infinite confusion of all values. There would be cynical Latins, and some man of Freud's from Vienna. Articulate among them would be the great Jung, bland, supervigorous, on his rounds

between the forests of anthropology and the neuroses of school-boys. At first there would be an American cast to the congress, almost Rotarian in its forms and ceremonies, then the closer-knit European vitality would fight through, and finally the Americans would play their trump card, the announcement of colossal gifts and endowments, of great new plants and training-schools, and in the presence of the figures the Europeans would blanch and walk timidly.

The relation of Europe to America, as Fitzgerald conceives of it, is perfectly represented in this passage. It is a combination of financial dependency and intellectual contempt. Compared to the sophistication that has become second nature even to otherwise mediocre Europeans, America is little more than a gigantic "nursery" (the word is Fitzgerald's). America, as he sees it, is the home of eternal optimism, based on nothing more substantial than illusions—illusions, for example, "of the essential goodness of people" which originally sprang out of "the lies of generations of frontier mothers who had to croon falsely that there were no wolves outside the cabin door." Dick Diver's friend and colleague, Franz, in spite of his respect for Dick's intelligence and real talent in psychiatry, sees in him "the same unaging American face." Doctor Diver is capable enough, of course, to recognize his own limitations. When he first comes to Europe and associates with Elkins, a member of the American embassy personnel, he sees in this man a faint reflection of some national quality in himself and it is hardly a flattering one: "Elkins . . . would name you all the quarterbacks at New Haven for thirty years." (Fitzgerald, in *The Crack-Up,* was to confess in the first person singular that almost to the end of his life, his most persistent daydream was that of being the hero of the Princeton football squad.) Dick Diver, as a student in Europe, begins to doubt the quality of his mental processes and to mock his own reasoning power, "calling it specious and 'American'—his criterion of uncerebral phrasemaking was that it was American."

Franz regards Dick Diver as something of a genius, but it is not his genius that interests him quite as much as his connection with the Warren fortune. He approaches his friend with the idea of opening a psychiatric clinic in Switzerland: " 'There we have it! Money!' he bewailed, 'I have little money. The price in American money is two hundred thousand dollars. . . . But the clinic is a gold mine— I tell you, I have seen the books. . . .' " Dick turns to his sister-in-law, "Baby" Warren and asks: "In your experience, Baby, have you found that when a European wants to see an American *very* pressingly it is invariably something concerned with money?" The deal goes through, but it eventually comes to a bad end when Dick begins to imbibe alcohol a little too freely and so convinces Franz's wife and then Franz himself that he is no longer a "serious" person and that the days of his creative accomplishment in medicine are over. (Drinking heavily, to judge from *Tender Is the Night,* was the great and constant activity of Americans in Europe during the Prohibition period described. Abe North, the promising composer who peters out in alcoholism, is the representative example. He returns to his native country only for the *coup de grâce:* he is beaten to death in a New York speakeasy.)

Dick's attitude toward material things, like so much else about him, is essentially contradictory. Fitzgerald captures this quality when he remarks that the effect of Dick's witnessing (during his boyhood) the economic struggles of his father had been to wed "a desire for money to an essentially unacquisitive nature." His marriage to the fabulously wealthy Nicole, we must suppose, is a result of this contradiction and an aggravation of it. He thinks of himself bitterly at times as a kind of gigolo swallowed up by the Warren fortune. Yet it is for this very reason that he takes care to retain his financial independence of his wife. He has inherited a small income of $3000 a year and this is augmented by royalties that "dribble in" from his two textbooks which had created a stir in psychiatry when they first appeared. He calculated his share of the cost in his domestic economy, paying for his son's education and "living rather ascetically, travelling third class when he was alone, with the cheapest wine and good care of his clothes." In this way, he tries to maintain the fiction of "a qualified independence." The qualification is due to his wife's wealth—an "income (which) had increased so fast of late that it seemed to belittle his work." They cannot help living like rich people, yet Dick never escapes for very long the thought of his dilemma when using her money. When he goes to the bank, he is asked "whether he wanted to draw upon his wife's money or his own." Eventually he comes to feel that somehow "he had lost himself—he could not tell the hour when or the day or the week, the month or the year."

The contrast between the heiress Nicole and the Hollywood actress, Rosemary, as others have noted before, is the contrast between inherited wealth and earned income. Rosemary, no matter how much she actually earns, can never forget that she has worked hard for her money (even, on one memorable occasion, risked her life for it).

The result is obvious. Nicole spends with an abandon and insouciance that Rosemary may admire but can never hope to emulate. "Nicole was sure that the money she spent was hers—Rosemary still thought her money was miraculously lent to her and she must consequently be very careful of it."

We recognize in the distinction between Nicole and Rosemary one that had already been made in *The Great Gatsby*. In that earlier novel, the distinction had been summed up in the difference between East Egg (the home of hereditary wealth) and West Egg (the home of the self-made and newly rich). Rosemary economizes compulsively because she is captive to the habit of doing so. She cannot possibly acquire the carefree attitude of Nicole:

> With Nicole's help Rosemary bought two dresses and two hats and four pairs of shoes with her money. Nicole bought from a great list that ran to two pages, and bought the things in the windows besides. Everything she liked that she couldn't possibly use herself, she bought as a present for a friend. She bought colored beads, folding beach cushions, artificial flowers, honey, a guest-bed, bags, scarfs, love birds, miniatures for a doll's house, and three yards of some new cloth the color of prawns. She bought a dozen bathing suits, a rubber alligator, a travelling chess set of gold and ivory, big linen handkerchiefs for Abe, two chamois leather jackets of kingfisher blue and burning bush from Hermes. . . .

This lavishness and generosity is associated by Fitzgerald not with display (as it might be if the person indulging in such spending were newly rich) but with the quality of being a great lady, rather than a very highly paid working girl like Rosemary. Hollywood, which Rosemary represents in this novel, is treated patronizingly by Fitzgerald, in a way that foreshadows, at least in part, his treatment of it in his next and last novel, *The Last Tycoon*. Hollywood is blighted by the insecurity and vulgarity traditionally associated with the concept of the *nouveau riche*. Yet it only reflects the shortcomings of the society which has adopted it as its expression.

Hollywood people, like all people who are basically insecure in a psychological sense, never quite feel equal to the people around them but feel instead alternately very much above them or very much below them. In the end, however, it is the feeling of self-esteem that prevails over their gnawing doubts. They think of themselves as "people of bravery and industry; they were risen to a position of prominence in a nation which for a decade had wanted only to be entertained."

Rosemary takes the initiative in arranging a screen test for Dick without any sense of incongruity or intention of insult. She just naturally assumes that it is the dream of every American, no matter how rich or intellectual or influential, to "get into the movies." And though she is wrong about Dick, she is not so far off in her calculations as far as the other characters are concerned. Nicole, for example, is hurt because she has not been thought worthy of a screen test. Hollywood here supplies a new standard of aristocracy. Just as Proust's ultrafashionable and exclusive Duchesse de Guermantes eventually comes to associate with actresses of questionable antecedents in the general collapse of social values in the Faubourg Saint-Germain following World War I, so Fitzgerald shows us that there are no greater "ladies" in our modern world than those whose images are flashed on screens of darkened movie houses or (more recently) on our television screens.

From the point of view of art, Hollywood is, for the most part, incredibly childish. Rosemary's masterpiece is entitled *Daddy's Girl*, and Fitzgerald's description of it shows that the title was merited: "Daddy's girl. Was it a 'itty-bitty bravekins' and did it suffer? Ooo-ooo-tweet, de tweetest thing, wasn't she dest too tweet? Before her tiny fist the forces of lust and corruption rolled away; nay, the very march of destiny stopped, inevitable became evitable; syllogism, dialectic, all rationality fell away. Women would forget the dirty dishes at home and weep; even within the picture one woman wept so long that she almost stole the film away from Rosemary. She wept all over a set that cost a fortune."

But if one side of American life in the first quarter of the twentieth century was labeled "Sentimentality," the other side was labeled "Violence." America between the two world wars (and particularly in the decade of the lush 1920s) was the land of Hemingway's "killers," of Jay Gatsby, of Prohibition, and gang-land rule. That was the land from which Dick Diver, Abe North, and other expatriates escaped and to which they eventually were compelled to return to face their own destruction. The delicate, sensitive intellectual who suddenly succumbs to his emotions and strikes out indiscriminately against a world he has lost control of and succeeds only in getting much the worst of the exchange that follows—is a theme that fascinated Fitzgerald. In *The Beautiful and Damned*, the reader had been compelled to watch in horror while Anthony Patch was beaten half to death. In *Tender Is the Night*, Dick Diver suffers the same fate. It is only "Baby" Warren's masterful influence that gets him out of the clutches of the Italian Fascist police after they have administered a terrible beating to him. But Dick himself had initially been responsible for starting the fight, incited to it by an insatiable pride, that is viewed almost as a national characteristic. A difference of opinion between Dick and an Italian cab driver about an overcharge precipitates the hero's near-destruction: "The passionate impatience of the weak leaped up in Dick and clothed itself like a flash in violence, the honorable, the traditional resource of his land; he stepped forward and clipped the man's face."

But America is not the only target of Fitzgerald's satire in this book. England and Englishmen are denigrated time after time: "(Dick) found something antipathetic in the English lately. England was like a rich man after a disastrous orgy who makes up to the household by chatting with them individually, when it is obvious to them that he is only trying to get back his self-respect in order to usurp his former power." The French do not appear in any more sympathetic light. Nor are the various Negroes, who appear in a series of scenes revolving around Abe North, handled sympathetically. As for the family of Von Cohn Morris, the Australian patient at Dick's clinic, its members are about as abominable and aggressive, individually and collectively, as the relatives of Meyer Wolfsheim (who took over Jay Gatsby's household in the declining phase of his career) had been in the earlier novel.

The complete list of objects toward which Fitzgerald directs his irritability rivals the one he himself compiled in *The Crack-Up* (referring to a period of time which must have come on the heels of the one in which *Tender Is the Night* was written): "In those latter days I couldn't stand the sight of Celts, English, Politicians, Strangers, Virginians, Negroes (light or dark), Hunting People, or retail clerks and middlemen in general, all writers (I avoided writers very carefully because they can perpetuate trouble as no one else can)— and all the classes as classes and most of them as members of their class."

Of all the darts aimed in this novel, however, those aimed at America, Americans, and American civilization in general are the deadliest and most numerous. And generally, the most effective mockery of things American comes not from the Europeans in the cast but from Americans themselves. It is only rarely that a European in the story is allowed to voice his criticism. A good example of the latter is supplied by Dick Diver's associate Franz Gergorovius —the psychiatrist—on the subject of the American penchant for popularizing esoteric knowledge. Dick's first little book is to be entitled "A Psychology for Psychiatrists," and Franz approves of it ironically in the following fashion: "All right, you are an American. You can do this without professional harm. I do not like these generalities. Soon you will be writing little books called 'Deep Thoughts For The Layman,' so simplified that they are positively guaranteed not to cause thinking. If my father were alive, he would look at you and grunt, Dick."

Fitzgerald implies that each is right, but that his point of view permits him only to see his neighbor's defects, not his own. The Europeans in the story are spongers at the feast prepared for them by Americans, and they show not the slightest gratitude to their benefactors once their usefulness is ended. Franz shows little hesitation in dropping his friend Dick from part-ownership of their clinic once his financial support becomes superfluous. As a matter of fact, the shabby treatment he receives at the end seems to justify Dick's cynicism in the beginning. The cynicism is evident in the brutally realistic terms in which he explains Franz's proposal to his sister-in-law "Baby" Warren: "This young Private-dozent thinks that he and I ought to launch into big business and try to attract nervous breakdowns from America."

The weakness of the novel as a whole cannot be detected readily in any of the details, because they are disguised by some very effective writing. The failure is an over-all one of form. If this novel has some of the qualities of a precious gem, it still lacks those of the consummate art evident in *The Great Gatsby*. No intermittent phosphorescence can compensate for the absence of the brilliant and steady illumination of that masterwork. The author in this case did not clearly define his artistic purpose as he had in his previous novel and the result is expressionistic in the derogatory sense. The writing is a response to pressures within Fitzgerald himself, which were rapidly building up to an explosion. These pressures prevented him from exercising fully the kind of control that an artist needs in order to produce a "thing of beauty" that is something more than merely a document possessing some significance and some truth. The result is a schism in the story that was perceived at once by readers and reviewers alike and one which now, after a quarter of a century of discussion and re-examination, still makes *Tender Is the Night*, despite all its detailed excellences, second-best among Fitzgerald's works.

5

THE LAST TYCOON

I N "A NOTE ON FITZGERALD" which is reprinted in *The Crack-Up*, John Dos Passos discusses *The Last Tycoon*. He regards this unfinished novel as "of sufficient dimensions to raise the level of American fiction to follow in some such way as Marlowe's blank verse line raised the whole level of Elizabethan verse." In Dos Passos' mind, this mere fragment and skeletal outline of a book managed even more successfully than *The Great Gatsby* "to weld together the two divergent halves, to fuse the conscientious worker that no creative man can ever really kill with the moneyed celebrity who aimed his stories at the twelve-year-olds." In the same vein, Edmund Wilson, in his Introduction to the *Tycoon*, claims that "even in its unfulfilled intention [it] takes its place among the books that set a standard."

Dos Passos has even more remarkable things to say:

It is tragic that Scott Fitzgerald did not live to finish *The Last Tycoon*. Even as it stands I have an idea that it will turn out to be one of those literary fragments that from time to time appears in the stream of a culture and profoundly influences the course of future events. His unique achievement, in these beginnings of a great novel, is that here for the first time he has managed to establish that unshakable moral attitude towards the world we live in and towards its temporary standards that is the basic essential of any powerful work of the imagination. A firmly anchored ethical standard is something that American writing has been struggling towards for half a century.

Expanding this thesis later in the essay, Dos Passos adds:

This establishment of a frame of reference for common humanity has been the main achievement of writing which in other times and places has come to be called great. It requires as well as the necessary skill with the tools of the trade, secure standards of judgment that can only be called ethical. Hollywood, the subject of *The Last Tycoon*, is probably the most important and the most difficult subject for our time to deal with. Whether we like it or not it is in that great bargain sale of five and ten cent lusts and dreams that the new bottom level of our culture is being created. The fact that at the end of a life of brilliant worldly successes and crushing disasters Scott Fitzgerald was engaged so ably in a work of such importance proves him to have been the first-rate novelist his friends believed him to be. In *The Last Tycoon* he was managing to invent a set of people seen really in the round instead of lit by an envious spotlight from above or below. *The Great Gatsby* remains a perfect example of this sort of treatment at an earlier, more anecdotic stage, but in the fragments of *The Last Tycoon,* you can see the beginning of a real grand style.

In dealing with an unfinished work, we must, of course, distinguish between the intentions of the author and his actual achievement. We must further distinguish, in this particular case, among the author's various intentions, for Fitzgerald was anything but unified in mind and heart when he undertook this work, and different facets of his personality emerged in his plans.

Evidently, at the time he was beginning this novel, Fitzgerald himself felt that it would be a masterpiece. In a letter to his daughter, he says of the *Tycoon*: "Look! I've begun to write something that is maybe great, and I'm going to be absorbed in it four or six months. It may not make us a cent but it will pay expenses and it is the first labor of love I've undertaken since the first part of 'Infidelity.' Anyhow I'm alive again." But he may have been deluding himself about his spiritual state as much as he was about his physical one. It is possible to agree with William Troy when he says that *The Last Tycoon* "includes some of the most unfortunate writing Fitzgerald has left."

At the time he was writing this novel, he was more deeply involved with Hollywood than he thought, and so once again he failed to be objective or to keep his proper distance from his subject. This was an old story with Fitzgerald and the persistent cause of his artistic failures. In *This Side of Paradise,* he had been too deeply involved with the Princeton boys' Weltanschauung to do more than make passing criticisms of it; in *Tender Is the Night* he had succumbed to the attractions of the Mediterranean coterie he had been describing; in this last novel, written after his own "crack-up," he was less capable than ever of submitting a phenomenon such as Hollywood to any permanent standards of judgment.

In an outline of his novel which he prepared for the benefit of a magazine publisher in September 1939, there seems to be a clear indication of this incapacity: "We have a love affair between Stahr and Thalia [later this name was changed to Kathleen], an immediate, dynamic, unusual, physical love affair. . . . This love affair is the meat of the book." The point of view of the passage as well as the diction are undeniably those of Hollywood. One might say, then, that Fitzgerald was adapting his language to the recipient of the letter, and that he was emphasizing those angles of his work best calculated to appeal to a large American magazine audience. Undoubtedly this motivation entered into the scheme, but it is also clear that Fitzgerald was actually doing his best to deliver a story that would fit these specifications. He described the affair elsewhere as "very Hollywood." To see how well the finished work might have merited this description, we can look at a passage from the fifth chapter of the *Tycoon*:

> The house had dissolved a little back into its elements. They found the dripping beams of a doorway and groped over mysterious waist-high obstacles to the single finished room of sawdust and odorous wet wood. When he took her in his arms, they could just see each other's eyes in the half-darkness. Presently his raincoat dropped to the floor. "Wait," she said.
>
> She needed a minute. She did not see how any good could come from this, though this did not prevent her from being happy and desirous, she needed a minute to think how it was, to go back an hour and know how it happened. She waited in his arms, moving her head a little from side to side as she had before, only more slowly, and never taking her eyes from his. Then she discovered that he was trembling.
>
> He discovered it at the same time, and his arms relaxed. Immediately she spoke to him coarsely and provocatively, and pulled his face down to hers. Then, with her knees she struggled out of something, still standing up and holding him with one arm, and kicked it off beside the coat. He was not trembling now and he held her again, as they knelt down together and slid to the raincoat on the floor.

Reading such a description, there is little doubt that it was constructed to conform to the standard Hollywood definition of "an immediate, dynamic, unusual, physical love affair." The marked distaste which the passage arouses in the reader makes one agree with the critic who remarked that Fitzgerald was never at his best in attempting a *direct* depiction of sexual passion. Judging by the results in this case, it is fortunate that he does not try anything similar elsewhere in his work. Fitzgerald had evidently lived too long in Hollywood, and had succumbed to its influences. He thought he could rival the salacious suggestiveness of its performances; he would out-Hollywood Hollywood.

If Fitzgerald's notion that Stahr's love affair would eventually constitute "the meat" of his new book were true, the critical reader should probably have found it lean and tasteless fare indeed. But his instinct as a novelist to exploit the material that he could handle best led him in another direction which, had the work ever been completed, would have become increasingly dominant. More and more, his intention was to show the mechanism of the motion-picture business "from the inside." This phrase is not meant primarily to suggest the scabrous, the scandalous, or the "confidential"—though there is a swarm of all these elements in the book. (Two examples that readily come to mind in this connection are Wylie White's description of his affair with the wife of a producer who said to him as soon as it was over: "Don't you ever tell about this or I'll have you thrown out of Hollywood. My husband's a much more important man than you!"; and Cecilia's description of how she surprised her father in the midst of a hectic business day and found his secretary, Birdie Peters, completely nude in an airless cupboard into which he had stuffed her when he heard somebody at the door!) What is meant, instead, is that Fitzgerald was fascinated by the technical process of making films and he intended to share this interest with other Americans. He realized that very little interest existed in this area, even in those intellectual circles where for some unclear reason he apparently thought he was most likely to find it. Americans were, in general, prepared to take their movies, as they took their cars and other machines, pragmatically, that is, to make use of them for enjoyment but rarely (if ever) to look under the hoods to find out what made their wheels go round. That was for the specialists, the mechanics, the technicians.

But somewhere along the line, Fitzgerald, like an old-car enthusiast who putters around with an old motor until he knows how to take it apart and put it together again, had picked up the details of the *movie mechanism*. Like all enthusiasts with esoteric interests, he became firmly convinced that his interest in the subject was not something peculiar to himself but was latent in a great many people and he was prepared to do what he could to awaken it. This is the task he sets for himself in *The Last Tycoon*, and he goes about it with such energy, subtlety, and success that he merits the praise

73

given to him by Edmund Wilson on this score: "The moving-picture business in America has here been observed at a close range, studied with a careful attention and dramatized with a sharp wit such as are not found in combination in any of the other novels on the subject. *The Last Tycoon* is far and away the best novel we have had about Hollywood. . . ."

But this is faint praise indeed (the only serious competition for the distinction presumably might come from Nathanael West). Fitzgerald's reliance upon the technical aspect of the making of moving pictures as an important element of his work is an indication of how empty of humanly significant content he felt this book to be. Because he had nothing dramatically important to say about life as he had in some of his earlier books, the heart of *The Last Tycoon* is a moral vacuum, which must have been the counterpart of the vacuum in Fitzgerald's heart at the time he was writing the book.

For a long time he had the idea of making the hero of a novel a Hollywood cameraman. The first version of what was to become *Tender Is the Night* was to be about "a man named Francis Melarky, a movie technician who visited the Riviera with his possessive mother." In *The Last Tycoon,* the author appoints himself a public guide for a tour of the moving-picture studios, and he includes glimpses of what goes on behind the scenes such as no guided tour ever gives. There is, first of all, the description of a Hollywood "lot" at night: "Under the moon the back lot was thirty acres of fairyland—not because the locations really looked like African jungles and French chateaux and steamers at anchor and Broadway by night, but because they looked like the torn picture-books of childhood, like fragments of stories dancing in an open fire. I never lived in a house with an attic, but a back lot must be something like that, and at night of course in an enchanted distorted way, it all comes true."

Then there is the description of the processes that actually make the wheels go round:

"Mr. Stahr's Projection Room" was a miniature picture theater with four rows of overstuffed chairs. In front of the front row ran long tables with dim lamps, buzzers and telephones. Against the wall was an upright piano, left there since the early days of sound. The room had been redecorated and reupholstered only a year before, but already it was ragged again with work and hours.

Here Stahr sat at two-thirty and again at six-thirty watching the lengths of film taken during the day. There was often a savage tensity about the occasion—he was dealing with *faits accomplis*—the net result of months of buying, planning, writing and rewriting, casting, constructing, lighting, rehearsing and shooting—the fruit of brilliant hunches or of counsels of despair, of lethargy, conspiracy and sweat. At this point the tortuous manoeuvre was staged and in suspension— these were reports from the battle-line.

Beside Stahr, there were present the representatives of all the technical departments, together with the supervisors and unit managers of the pictures concerned. The directors did not appear at these showings—officially because few punches were pulled here as money ran out in silver spools. There had evolved a delicate staying away.

The staff was already assembled. Stahr came in and took his place quickly, and the murmur of conversation died away. As he sat back and drew his thin knee up beside him on the chair, the lights in the room went out. . . .

This passage is an example of the kind of details which Fitzgerald intended to use to a greater extent as he completed the novel. He describes one of the characters he was going to develop, a man named Robinson, in his notes for the story: "I would like this episode to give a picture of the work of a cutter, camera man or sound unit director in the making of such a thing as *Winter Carnival,* accenting the speed with which Robinson works, his reactions, why he is what he is instead of being the very high-salaried man which his technical abilities entitle him to be." He considered including some characters in his cast for no better reason than that they were integral elements of the Hollywood scene though not necessarily part of his particular story. One of his other notes reads as follows: "There is a place for a hint somewhere of a big agent, to complete the picture."

The intention that such a statement plainly presupposes was bound to be one of the weaknesses of the finished book. The background of a story ought to be sketched in just enough to provide the events and characters with a local habitation and a name. Realism or naturalism pursued for its own sake beyond this point becomes fetishistic. In Fitzgerald's best work, the background is held in check and does not distract from the attention that should go to the foreground of the story. In *The Great Gatsby,* Fitzgerald had not forgotten for a moment that though the mechanics of Prohibition and gangsterism might be interesting subjects in themselves they were not his subjects as a novelist. Fitzgerald never knew the gangster world of Gatsby as intimately as he knew the Hollywood of

Monroe Stahr. It is ironic, then, that in *The Last Tycoon* his specialized knowledge, instead of being an asset, became a handicap which he could not wholly overcome. In a novel, it must never be forgotten by either writer or reader that the primary interest centers upon the human beings whom the novelist creates and the situations in which they are involved. It is perhaps because Fitzgerald no longer felt so sure of himself, even on his home ground, that he allowed the purely expository elements of *The Last Tycoon* to predominate in its scheme.

But what of those ethical intentions discerned by Dos Passos in the book? It would be strange indeed if they were completely absent, for, as Fitzgerald had said, he was always aware of a tendency in himself "to preach to people in some acceptable form," and to look upon himself as something more than a mere entertainer (in which derogatory classification he included Cole Porter, Rodgers, Hart, and "all that gang"). His intentions along this line in *The Last Tycoon* are most obvious in some of the unrealized plans Fitzgerald had for the ending of the novel. There was to be an airplane crash in which Monroe Stahr and a number of Hollywood celebrities were to be killed in an obscure region of the Rocky Mountains, disappearing in the fall and buried under the snows of winter. The following spring the wreckage was to be found by three youngsters (two boys and a girl) of very different characters. Each of them was to discover mementos of a victim who resembled himself or herself. The girl, for example, was to find some of the belongings of a famous actress; one of the boys was to come across the effects of a crooked Hollywood character, while the most admirable and honest boy in the group, named Jim, was to find Monroe Stahr's briefcase. This scene evidently was to have several purposes: to show that the seeds of character, though maturing slowly, are already present in early youth; to show that the lives of men have unforeseen effects on the imaginations and lives of the following generation ("What a man owes to society," says Irving Babbitt, "is not his philanthropy but a good example.") In his notes, Fitzgerald cautioned himself that "this must be subtly done and not look too much like a parable or moral lesson, still the impression must be conveyed, but be careful to convey it once and not rub it in. If the reader misses it, let it go —don't repeat. Show Frances [the young girl who finds the dead actress' belongings] as malleable and amoral in the situation, but show a definite doubt on Jim's part, even from the first, as to whether there is fair dealing even to the dead." (This refers to the other boy's suggestion that they hide the fact that they have found the wreckage and then loot and strip the plane. The last phrase reminds us that in *The Great Gatsby,* too, the final touchstone for testing the moral value of the different characters was their capacity for the feeling of reverence that is expressed in "fair dealing even to the dead!" All Gatsby's guests, except for the narrator Nick and the nameless man identified as "Owl-eyes," failed the test by not attending his funeral. Like the ancient Greeks, Fitzgerald feels that outrage or honor can still be done to a man after he is dead. This is significant, for, according to them, anyone with any decent feelings will recognize that responsibility to a man does not end with his earthly life.

Fitzgerald was fearful of his own impulse to moralize. In his notes for the projected incident, he wrote: "I cannot be too careful not to rub this in or give it the substance or feeling of a moral tale." He decided finally to give "a bitter and acrid finish to the incident to take away any possible sentimental and moral stuff that may have crept into it." He need hardly have troubled himself on this score however, for he was unable to sustain any genuinely moral preoccupation in the portions of the story that are finished (or almost finished). *The Last Tycoon* is reminiscent of Fitzgerald's own caustic observation (in a letter to his daughter) concerning the work of Thomas Wolfe: "His awful secret transpires at every crevice—he did not have anything particular to say!" The passage about the airplane crash and its effect on the lives of the three young people who discover it, even if he had managed to write it, could not have changed materially this negative impression. Fitzgerald's idea of showing the inevitable betrayal of each succeeding generation's promises and hopes is not original. It had been done before—notably by Dreiser at the close of *An American Tragedy*—where we are shown Clyde Griffiths' nephew in very much the same position (as part of a group of itinerant street preachers and singers) as that occupied years before, by his ill-fated uncle. Life in America, these authors seem to say, is bound to follow the same pattern it has followed up to now, so long as the economic and social forces that mold the American character remain basically the same. This essentially is the message of both Dreiser and Fitzgerald.

In terms of character, Monroe Stahr is undoubtedly the most interesting creation in *The Last Tycoon*. Stahr was Fitzgerald's first attempt to draw "a great man" of our contemporary world, but the fact that he turns out to be a Hollywood version of a great man rather than one unconditionally great does not seem to have occurred to the author. Or perhaps he might have said that there was no such thing as a man unconditionally great. Each man perforce has to be measured by the relative yardstick of a definite time and place and as Fitzgerald would say, given the twentieth century, given America, given Hollywood—Monroe Stahr is our type of hero.

But Fitzgerald did not attempt a portrait of this "great contemporary man" all at once. He had been preparing for a long time to do a study of an autochthonous variety of the Superman. Like Nietzsche, he thought it unlikely that the Superman would appear in any traditional guise (Nietzsche had said that, though speculation was futile as to the exact shape this mythical character might take, his own idea was that the Superman, when he did appear on the historical stage, would resemble Cesare Borgia rather than Parsifal!). The Superman was bound to be a sorry simulacrum if he turned up in anything but an unexpected guise—and what guise could be more surprising than that of a Hollywood movie magnate? Fitzgerald saw Stahr at the same time as completely up-to-date and as a throwback to an earlier stage of the American system of private enterprise. Here was the true inheritor of the mantle of the earlier tycoons: Rockefeller, Vanderbilt, Ford, Harriman, Gould, Frick— the empire builders, the captains of industry and finance, the capitalists.

Fitzgerald's study of Stahr (whose name never appeared on pictures and was almost unknown to the public, which did not recognize the very real though completely dark "star" who, as the true creative and controlling power behind the scenes, was infinitely more important than the tinsel-bright ones that he made or broke at will) should be connected with his lifelong interest in Napoleon. In one of the letters to his daughter at Vassar he tells her that he has accumulated a small library of a hundred and fifty books dealing with Napoleon (who was so important, also, to Nietzsche and to Dostoevski's Raskolnikov—those other speculators on the nature of the Superman). From the beginning of his writing career he had been concerned with a definition of "the big man" in school and in the world. Amory Blaine, in *This Side of Paradise,* had said: "Oh, Lord, what a pleasure it used to be to dream I might be a really great dictator or writer or religious or political leader—and now even a Leonardo da Vinci or Lorenzo de Medici couldn't be a real old-fashioned bolt in the world. Life is too huge and complex. The

78

world is so overgrown that it can't lift its own fingers, and I was planning to be such an important finger."

To this Amory adds the observation: "You're mistaking this period when every nut is an individualist for a period of individualism. Wilson has only been powerful when he has represented; he's had to compromise over and over again." This is significant because it is essentially the same observation that Monroe Stahr makes when he is speaking to the English writer Boxley: "There's always some lousy condition. . . . Our condition is that we have to take people's own favorite folklore and dress it up and give it back to them." In other words, Hollywood's strength, like that of the democratic politician, is derived from the fidelity with which it *represents*. This does not keep Stahr from appearing to be a hero in the classic sense to the sympathetic Boxley: "He had been reading Lord Charnwood and he recognized that Stahr like Lincoln was a leader carrying on a long war on many fronts; almost single-handed he had moved pictures sharply forward through a decade, to a point where the content of the 'A production' was wider and richer than that of the stage. Stahr was an artist only, as Mr. Lincoln was a general, perforce and as a layman."

Between Amory Blaine in *This Side of Paradise,* who had dreamed of becoming a "big man," and Monroe Stahr in *The Last Tycoon,* who actually became one, Fitzgerald had created three other heroes: Anthony Patch, Jay Gatsby, and Dick Diver. How do they measure up to the requirements of the hero? Anthony Patch, making his way to the status of multimillionaire by the routes of inheritance and litigation, is hardly heroic in the author's eyes or in ours. Gatsby is, of course, like Stahr, a self-made man, but he has taken an illegitimate short cut to success, and even within his own little particular circle of the underworld, he is only the creature of the sinister Meyer Wolfsheim. Dick Diver has the makings of a first-rate hero but he is too troubled and burdened with his own neuroses to exploit his potentialities. So we are left finally with Monroe Stahr as the sole realization of the Napoleonic dream in the context of our contemporary world.

Monroe Stahr is also Fitzgerald's one full-length study of a subject that apparently always interested him a great deal—the Jew in America. Meyer Wolfsheim (who had been described by Edith Wharton, in a letter to Fitzgerald, as the "perfect Jew") is a subordinate and rather shadowy figure in *The Great Gatsby.* Upon Stahr, on the other hand, the pitiless light of publicity is always beating. The result, as might be expected, is that deficiencies of character are discovered under Stahr's exterior side by side with points of positive and admirable strength.

Stahr, in one of Fitzgerald's figures of speech, has "just managed to climb out of a thousand years of Jewry." For him, as for the other Jews of Hollywood, the emancipation from the ghetto and the large opportunities opening out before him are still heady and exciting novelties. As a reflective intellectual, Stahr is actively conscious of his own motivations in a way that his associates are not: "They were all talking with enthusiasm about a horse that had run very fast, and Mr. Marcus was the most enthusiastic of all. Stahr guessed that the Jews had taken over the worship of horses as a symbol—for years it had been the Cossacks mounted and the Jews on foot. Now the Jews had horses, and it gave them a sense of extraordinary well-being and power."

On a personal level, Stahr had started as a member of a gang of kids in the Bronx. Someone who knew him at that time tells the narrator how he would bark out of the corner of his mouth. Although he raised himself out of this mire, Stahr could not help carrying the stigmata of his origin with him all of his life. His education had consisted of a night-school course in stenography. During working hours in the studio, he occasionally falls into the tough Bronx "lingo" of his childhood and youth. When he does not seem to recognize the names of Aeschylus and Aristophanes, we are left uncertain as to whether his ignorance is pretended or real.

Now Stahr is perched at the very top of the world. As Kathleen, who had once been the mistress of an ex-king in Europe, tells him, he is much more a king than one who merely inherited his title. Fitzgerald describes the inner circle to which Stahr now belongs:

> Eleven men and their guest, Prince Agge, sat at lunch in the private dining room of the studio commissary. They were the money men— they were the rulers; and unless there was a guest, they ate in broken silence, sometimes asking questions about each other's wives and children, sometimes discharging a single absorption from the forefront of their consciousness. Eight out of the ten were Jews— five of the ten were foreign-born, including a Greek and an Englishman; and they had all known each other for a long time: there was a rating in the group, from old Marcus down to old Leanbaum, who had bought the most fortunate block of stock in the business and never was allowed to spend over a million a year producing.

All of them are self-made men, newcomers; Fitzgerald refers to Stahr at one point as a parvenu. He is the maker of an "empire"; he experiences a feeling of satisfaction with his own creation. Fitzgerald contrasts Stahr's satisfaction in his possessions with the satisfaction of those persons "who have merely gypped another person's empire away from them like the four great railroad kings of the coast." Like Napoleon, he has earned his triumph by his genuine abilities, financial and otherwise. When he had first been admitted to the circle of "the rulers,"—a boy wonder of twenty-two—he had been

> a money man among money men. . . . He had been able to figure costs in his head with a speed and accuracy that dazzled them—for they were not wizards or even experts in that regard, despite the popular conception of Jews in finance. They were content to look at Stahr for the sublimated auditing, and experience a sort of glow as if they had done it themselves, like rooters at a football game.

But Stahr has defects which are inseparable from his virtues. Most important of his defects is a certain coldness and self-centeredness: "He has had everything in life except the privilege of giving himself unselfishly to another human being." This shortcoming in Fitzgerald's eyes, however, seems to be less a personal characteristic than a racial one. In *The Crack-Up*, we find him commenting on his own changed aspect at the time of his breakdown: "You began by pretending to be kind (politeness). It pays so well that it becomes second-nature. Some people like Jews can't get past the artificiality of the first step."

It has been remarked before that Fitzgerald's attitude to Jews is problematical. William Barrett, for example, writes: "Mizener does not, it seems to me, deal adequately or even frankly with one fact that stares out at us from Fitzgerald's life and printed page: that he was never quite reconciled to being Irish, and never faced up to that racial self-hatred which afflicts the Irishman in America as powerfully as the Jew (the figure of the Jew, by the way, seems to have had a curious fascination for Fitzgerald's imagination)." Barrett seems to have hit on a significant analogy between the situation of the Jews in America and that of the Irish. Fitzgerald certainly must have been aware of the resemblances between the two groups, as can readily be seen from the following passage in *The Beautiful and Damned*: "Jewesses were coming out into a society of Jewish men and women from Riverside to the Bronx, and looking forward to a rising young broker or jeweler and a kosher wedding; Irish girls were casting their eyes with license at last to do so, upon a society of young Tammany politicians, pious undertakers, and grown-up choir-boys."

Fitzgerald suffered a sense of alienation from America because of his Irish Catholic background. In *The Crack-Up*, he tells us that "when I was young, the boys in my street still thought that Catholics drilled in the cellar every night with the idea of making Pius the Ninth autocrat of this republic." And in a letter Fitzgerald wrote during the First World War he says: "Updike from Oxford or Harvard says: 'I die for England' or 'I die for America'—not me. I'm too Irish for that—I may get killed for America but I'm going to die for myself."

If Fitzgerald chooses to concentrate his attention on Jewish characters more often than on the Irish, it is possibly because he hoped in this way to be more objective in his attitude. The reason may be similar to the one which impelled him to make the narrator in *The Great Gatsby* a Yale man instead of a Princeton one like himself. A slight shift of that kind, trifling as it may appear to be, has the effect of simultaneously setting free and disciplining the imagination of the writer. In the works of Proust, as in those of Fitzgerald, there are also minor changes from autobiographical fact, and the explanation for such changes is the same in both instances. It was Fitzgerald's ambivalence of feeling about the Irish, the Jews, and himself that enabled him to identify so completely with Monroe Stahr and thus to go from the creation of Meyer Wolfsheim, the despicable villain in *Gatsby*, to that of Stahr, the great and heroic figure of *The Last Tycoon*.

Fitzgerald had, in *The Beautiful and Damned*, portrayed a Hollywood producer—Bloekman (who later in the novel changes his name to Joseph Black), vice-president of Films Par Excellence. Bloekman is not merely a Jew but a foreign-born Jew. A more obnoxious, aggressive, or abominable character, unless it is Meyer Wolfsheim, is hard to find in Fitzgerald's fiction. Bloekman had been "born in Munich [and] had begun his American career as a peanut vender with a traveling circus. At eighteen he was a sideshow ballyhoo." Like Meyer Wolfsheim (who had expressed such profound reverence for "Oggsford College"), and like Stahr himself for that matter, Bloekman has neither education nor culture. The feelings of injured vanity and impotent envy make him adopt a needling tone towards those more fortunate in this respect than himself. His tone is that of Wolfsheim when he says: "You college men? Harvard, eh. I see the Princeton boys beat you fellows at hockey." His feelings of inferiority impel him to "introduce himself with a little too evident assurance" and he is greeted with "a faint and ironic chill."

Bloekman plays a small but vivid role in *The Beautiful and Damned*. The heroine Gloria Patch treats him with about the same amount of consideration as Lady Brett Ashley shows to Robert Cohn in *The Sun Also Rises*. As for Anthony Patch, he is physically beaten on one occasion by Bloekman as badly as Dick Diver is beaten by the Italian Fascist police. Anthony, while drunk, had made the mistake of calling him "You Goddam Jew." Bloekman when questioned about the fight says merely that he hit Anthony because he was attempting to "blackmail him." Anthony is always extremely conscious of Jews; he identifies them in the streets by their offensive manners: "Two young Jewish men passed him, talking in loud voices and craning their necks here and there in fatuous, supercilious glances. They were dressed in suits of exaggerated tightness then semi-fashionable, their turned-over collars were notched at the Adam's apple; they wore gray spats and carried gray gloves on their cane handles."

Anthony, brooding over New York from the windows of an elevated train, makes some of the most interesting and significant observations to be found in Fitzgerald's work on the Jew in the modern world:

> Down in a tall busy street he read a dozen Jewish names on a line of stores; in the door of each stood a dark little man watching the passers from intent eyes—eyes gleaming with suspicion, with pride, with clarity, with cupidity, with comprehension. New York—he could not dissociate it now from the slow, upward creep of this people— the little stores, growing, expanding, consolidating, moving, watched over with hawk's eyes and a bee's attention to detail. They slathered out on all sides. It was impressive—in perspective it was tremendous.

Anthony rents his apartment from a profiteering Jew and gets a close-up of him as a business operator:

> When he had first rented the rooms they had been mere potentialities, scarcely to be discerned at first, but Anthony had seen into these potentialities and arranged in the lease that he and the landlord should each spend a certain amount in improvements. Rent had gone up in the past four years and last year when Anthony had

waived his option, the landlord, a Mr. Sohenberg, had realized that he could get a much higher price for what was now a prepossessing apartment. Accordingly, when Anthony approached him on the subject in September he was met with Sohenberg's offer of a three-year lease at $2,500 a year (he had been paying $1,700). This, it seemed to Anthony, was outrageous. It meant that well over a third of their income would be consumed in rent. In vain he argued that his own money, his own ideas on the partitioning, had made the rooms attractive. . . . In vain he offered two thousand dollars. Mr. Sohenberg was obdurate. It seemed that two other gentlemen were considering it, just that sort of apartment was in demand for the moment, and it would scarcely be business to *give* it to Mr. Patch. Besides, though he had never mentioned it before, several of the other tenants had complained of the singing and dancing late at night, that sort of thing. . . . Inwardly raging Anthony hurried back to the Ritz to report his discomfiture to Gloria.

Anthony comes across Jews in all stages of the assimilatory process. There is, for example, the very advanced case of Rachel Jerryl, who is described as "an exquisitely dressed Jewess with dark hair and a lovely milky pallor. She seemed shy and vague, and these two qualities accentuated a rather delicate charm that floated about her. Her family were 'Episcopalians,' owned three smart women's shops along Fifth Avenue, and lived in a magnificent apartment on Riverside Drive. . . ."

But if Jews are unavoidable in New York, they *are* Hollywood, or at least the motion picture industry in Hollywood. We have already seen that of those whom Fitzgerald labeled "the rulers" of the industry there, eighty percent were Jews and fifty percent were foreign born. Monroe Stahr, of course, is a vast improvement upon Bloekman (or Black, "the moving pictureman"). His very name indicates an aspiration toward higher things, even as Black's name had pointed to an entire absence of spiritual quality. But when we examine him more closely, we see that Stahr is a twentieth-century Superman to Fitzgerald mainly because he is an amoralist who has passed "beyond good and evil."

What is it precisely that has given Stahr his great insight into our time? Fitzgerald sums it up in a well-known figure of speech: "He had flown up very high to see, on strong wings, when he was young. And while he was up there he had looked on all the kingdoms, with the kind of eyes that can stare straight into the sun. Beating his wings tenaciously—finally frantically—and keeping on beating them, he had stayed up there longer than most of us, and then, remembering all he had seen from his great height of how things were, he had settled gradually to earth."

Stripped of its romantic verbiage, this means only that Stahr was able to see the direction in which his epoch was moving and to add his particular push in the same direction. And Fitzgerald seems to admire this quality. He is contemptuous of opportunists on a small scale (like the director Reinmund, for example) but sympathetic to the opportunist of Napoleonic dimensions. In this connection, it is possible to suggest an interpretation of the visit by airplane passengers to the Hermitage of Andrew Jackson described at the beginning of the story. It symbolizes, perhaps, the real beginnings of a triumphant, vulgar democracy in America. Begin with Andrew Jackson and you are bound to end with Hollywood.

Hollywood has taken upon itself the task of giving back to the people their own myths, of *representing* them without inquiring too deeply into the worth of what is being represented. If Fitzgerald has any moral standard to suggest in this book, other than that of Nietzsche, it is the closely related one of Spengler (Kathleen tells Stahr that her European lover, the king who had been "out of a job," had hoped to teach her the meaning of Spengler's philosophy). Spengler had chosen as the epigraph of his study of the decline of the West the Latin motto: *Fata volentem ducunt, nolentem trahunt.*[1] Stahr is not only one of the willing ones of this world, he is one of the eager and farsighted ones of his epoch. He does not conceive it to be his job to judge his time or to stand up against it when he thinks that it may be on the wrong track. The time, as Pound put it in "Mauberley," demanded "an image of its accelerated grimace." Men like Stahr helped supply that image and men like Fitzgerald, though they had the education and intelligence to know better, admired them for the huge successes they gained at the box office by catering to the appetites of a sensation-hunting public.

Fitzgerald compared contemporary America to ancient Rome, probably in her decline. One of the witticisms popular with intellectuals in the 1920s was that the United States was the only country in history ever to go from barbarism to decadence without passing through the stage of civilization. Monroe Stahr regards himself as something of a classical Roman. In an argument with the communist organizer Brimmer which ends in a fist fight (and could

---

[1] The Fates lead the willing and drag the unwilling.

end only in a fight) because Stahr's mind is absolutely closed against Communism, the producer says: "I never thought that I had more brains than a writer has. But I always thought that his brains *belonged* to me—because I knew how to use them. Like the Romans —I've heard that they never invented things but they knew what to do with them. Do you see? I don't say it's right. But it's the way I've always felt—since I was a boy."

Stahr is described as a conservative, paternalistic employer: "Success had come to him young, at twenty-three, and left certain idealisms of his youth unscarred." Though he had begun as a "money-man," he is a worker, too. He is always ready, if need be, to take off his coat and go to work, whereas Cecilia's father and Stahr's partner in business (who eventually tries to have him murdered) "is not interested in the making of pictures save as it will benefit his bank account." Despite his faults (the most serious fault is the coldness of temperament which makes him the last in a long train of causes that drive the producer Manny Schwartz to suicide) Stahr appears to be the comparatively hopeful figure in Hollywood. But Fitzgerald came to the pessimistic conclusion that he was something of a forlorn hope. The labor unions, the unscrupulous money-men who have no interest in making good pictures, the outright gangsters, seem to him to be taking over there as everywhere else in America. Fitzgerald's notes indicate that he would have attempted to show this had he lived to complete the novel. The crash of Stahr's plane was to be emblematic of another fall as well. He was to be "the last tycoon," the last wholly independent man. He had come out of nowhere in the beginning of his life, and he was destined to plunge into nothingness at the end. In other words, he was to illustrate the same philosophy of nihilistic existentialism which Fitzgerald had outlined more abstractly in *The Crack-Up*—that life at best is merely a trajectory between zero and zero.

6

OTHER WRITINGS—
FITZGERALD'S CONFESSIONS:
THE CRACK-UP

W HEN FITZGERALD remarked in the second installment of *The Crack-Up* in *Esquire* magazine that "there are always those to whom all self-revelation is contemptible," he may have been thinking of friends such as Ernest Hemingway, or he may have been thinking of himself as he had been at one time. In any case, he certainly seems ill at ease in speaking to the public in the first person singular. He was more used to addressing his audience from behind the mask of either the impersonal narrator or else the hero who, although differing from Fitzgerald in the outward circumstances of his life, inwardly resembled him.

An article by Dwight Taylor published in a 1959 issue of *Harper's* gives a valuable insight into Fitzgerald's method of transforming fact into fiction. Taylor indicates the precise proportion of reality to invention in Fitzgerald's short story "Crazy Sunday," which is based upon an incident that took place in Hollywood involving both men. Their respective roles in the story were the reverse of those that they enacted in real life. In other words, *fact turned inside out* is the formula for this particular fiction, as, indeed, it is of much fiction. Fitzgerald was apparently able to achieve free play of his imaginative powers by projecting his own feelings of guilt and embarrassment upon a character whom he does not consciously identify as himself.

Whether or not he felt that in *The Crack-Up* he had at last summoned up the courage to turn the "white light" on his heart, he has produced in this fragmentary work an important addition to the highest type of confessional literature. It was once said of Rousseau's *Confessions* that "if [he] had held his tongue he might have stood lower as a man of letters. . . ." That is to say, Rousseau, despite his prolific literary production in a number of forms, did not write anything more significant or interesting than his confessions. The same thing, however, can hardly be said of Fitzgerald. His genius lay more in the sphere of dramatization than in direct self-revelation. Yet he was so fine a writer and his subject in *The Crack-Up* is so unusual and important that he produced a highly meaningful and, in some ways, a great work.

The confessional form itself deserves some comment before discussing Fitzgerald's successes and failures in meeting its demands. A confession is more or less a lengthy soliloquy, and though it seem the easiest form to write (as *free verse,* to the inexperienced, seems the easiest of forms), it is, in reality most difficult. Truth is valuable because it is so rare; it takes power, persistence, and patience to reach it, to dig beneath the accumulated crust of habit and convention to where it lies hidden, even from oneself.

The touchstone of truth, when it is encountered in the confession, is the pain it gives. The truth does hurt; it hurts both finder and reader. (We cannot read Saint Augustine's or Rousseau's confessions without becoming aware of how destructive it must have been to the writer's ego and perhaps even his self-respect when he became *aware* of his own internal deficiencies, even apart from his decision to share this awareness with other people.) For the writer, the public takes the place of the priest or the psychoanalyst to whom he reveals the record of his maleficent thoughts, words, or deeds. The confession is useless unless there is an element of real contrition in it. It should lay bare the deepest, most unspeakable sources of a man's difficulties. A literary confession not purchased at the price of affliction, anguish, self-torture is useless, both for the writer and the reader. It must go to the root of the trouble, or, to use the Psalmist's expression, it must reveal the "truth even unto its innermost parts." Most writers fail because they are too ashamed to disclose, even to themselves, what they are like beneath their refined, civilized exterior.

For this reason some have held that a true confession—that is, one in which posturing and self-dramatization do not predominate —is an impossibility. We read in James Huneker's essay on Baudelaire, for example, that "notwithstanding his desperate effort to realize Poe's idea, he only proved Poe correct, who had said that no man can bare his heart quite naked; there will be always something held back, something false too ostentatiously thrust forward. The grimace, the attitude, the pomp of rhetoric are so many buffers between the soul of man and the sharp reality of published confessions." And in Dostoevski's *Notes from Underground,* a thinly disguised but most remarkable confession, we read:

> I want to try the experiment whether one can, even with oneself, be perfectly open and not take fright at the whole truth. I will observe, in parenthesis, that Heine says that a true autobiography is almost an impossibility, and that man is bound to lie about himself. He considers that Rousseau certainly told lies about himself in his confessions, and even intentionally lied, out of vanity. I am convinced that Heine is right; I quite understand how sometimes one may out of sheer vanity, attribute regular crimes to oneself, and indeed I can very well conceive that kind of vanity.

Judged by the standards suggested by these reflections, how does Fitzgerald's work rank? Glenway Wescott's answer to this question in an essay which he called "The Moral of Scott Fitzgerald" is that it should rank very high indeed:

> In 1936, in three issues of *Esquire,* he published the autobiographical essay, *The Crack-Up,* as it were his swan-song. . . . There is very little in world literature like this piece. . . . The great thing about Fitzgerald was his candor; verbal courage; simplicity. One little man with eyes really witnessing; objective in all he uttered, even about himself in a subjective slump. . . . The thing, I think, that a number of recent critics have most disliked about him is his confessional way, the personal tone, the tête-à-tête or man-to-man style, first person singular. . . . I on the other hand feel a real approval and emulation of just that; and I recommend that all our writers give it serious consideration. It might be the next esthetic issue and new mode of American letters. It is American enough; our greatest fellows, such as Franklin and Audubon and Thoreau and Whitman, were self-expressers in so far as they knew themselves. . . . I suggest revelation of man as he appears to himself in his mirror—not as he poses or wishes or idealizes—as one thing to try a revival of, this time. Naked truth about man's nature in unmistakable English. . . . And for clarity's sake, let us often use, and sanction the use of, words of one syllable. The shortest and most potent is the personal pronoun: I.

This high estimate of the literary value of Fitzgerald's confession is sustained by Edouard Roditi in his introduction to the French translation, *Gatsby le magnifique.* He says in it: *"The Crack-Up* on ne peut comparer qu'a *l'Aurélia* de Nerval, à la *Saison en Enfer* de

Rimbaud, au *De Profundis* d'Oscar Wilde, ou au debut de la Matinée chez la Princesse de Guermantes dans *Le Temps Retrouvé.*" [1] However, the kind of expectations built up by such sympathetic criticism as that of Glenway Wescott or Roditi are somewhat exaggerated and likely to lead to disappointment. Though very superior indeed by more modest standards, it just is not as good as they suggest. There are deficiencies in it purely as confession. It does not contain enough close-ups of actual experience. The minute and painfully remembered details—such as the incident involving the comb which Rousseau was accused of breaking or the incident involving the theft of the ribbon which he blamed upon an innocent servant— are lacking in *The Crack-Up*. Even if one agrees that the best writing in this form relates to the life that it chronicles as shadow does to substance, or as smoke to fire, still (to pursue the latter figure) there is a difference between the smoke which is still intermixed with flame and the smoke that simply marks the spot where a fire has gone out. The greatest confessional writing contains more concrete evidence than does *The Crack-Up* that its author was burned in the fire of reality. No doubt Fitzgerald found himself immolated in such a fire once, but the precise point at which the flame entered into him has been forgotten (or, at least, not revealed) and only the general impression of excruciating pain has remained.

This impression is communicated mainly through intellectual generalizations. These generalizations are lucid and brilliantly quotable: "In a real dark night of the soul it is always three o'clock in the morning, day after day." "The natural state of the sentient adult is a qualified unhappiness." "Trouble has no necessary connection with discouragement—discouragement has a germ of its own, as different from trouble as arthritis is different from a stiff joint." "It occurred to me that of all natural forces, vitality is the incommunicable one." These concentrated aphorisms seem to be at a comparatively high intellectual level, and there are an extraordinary number of such sentences crowded into relatively few pages.

The disadvantage of a brilliant style for the confessional form is that almost imperceptibly, it shades off occasionally into mere rhetoric. Rhetoric, like sentimentality, seeps in whenever true feeling fails for any reason. Behind rhetoric, as behind sentimentality, one may be conscious of feeling, but it is remembered feeling, "recon-

---

[1] "*The Crack-Up* can only be compared to *Aurélia* by Gerard de Nerval, *A Season in Hell* by Rimbaud, *De Profundis* by Wilde, and the beginning of the Princesse de Guermantes' afternoon party in Proust's *Past Recaptured.*"

sidered passion." And the memory, compensating for present defi-
ciency, exaggerates what is already past. That is why nostalgia is
so deceptive in its quality. Thus, true feeling is more likely to
express itself in restraint and understatement than it is in full-blown
rhetoric.

In Fitzgerald's case, the real emotions and ideas of his confession
have to be read through an obscuring mist of verbal artifice. What
emerges as the essence of his personal philosophy at this low point
in his spiritual life is a sort of existentialism or nihilistic despair
resembling that which became fashionable in Europe in the wake
of World War II. This is the philosophy which seems to permeate
such a passage as the following (especially perhaps the concluding
phrases):

> Life, ten years ago, was largely a personal matter. I must hold in
> balance the sense of the futility of effort and the sense of the
> necessity to struggle, the conviction of the inevitability of failure
> and still the determination to "succeed"—and, more than these,
> the contradiction between the dead hand of the past and the high
> intentions of the future. If I could do this through the common
> ills—domestic, professional, and personal—then *the ego would con-
> tinue as an arrow shot from nothingness to nothingness with such
> force that only gravity would bring it to earth at last.*[2]

"Out of nowhere into nothing" is Fitzgerald's view of life. One
can see why, if this view be true, everything should be permitted—
even cynicism and shamelessness. And indeed the closing section of
The Crack-Up is about as cynical a piece of writing as our time has
produced—genuinely cynical, not merely melodramatically so (like
some of the writing of the so-called beat generation). Fitzgerald in
this passage addresses his reader directly:

> If you are young and you should write asking to see me and learn
> how to be a sombre literary man writing pieces upon the state of
> emotional exhaustion that often overtakes writers in their prime—
> if you should be so young and so fatuous as to do this, I would not
> do so much as acknowledge your letter, unless you were related to
> someone very rich and important indeed. . . . I do not any longer
> like the postman, nor the grocer, nor the editor, nor the cousin's
> husband, and he in turn will come to dislike me, so that life will
> never be very pleasant again, and the sign *Cave Canem* is hung

[2] Italics added by author.

permanently just above my door. I will try to be a correct animal though, and if you throw me a bone with enough meat on it I may even lick your hand.

It may be passages like this that Glenway Wescott had in mind when he amended his admiration for *The Crack-Up* with the observation: "Indeed it is cheap here and there, but in embarrassment rather than in crudity or lack of courage." Cynicism, it has been said, is often romanticism gone sour. There is little doubt that in Fitzgerald cynicism is simply his youthful "idealism" turned inside out. He shows a sharp ability to penetrate into himself and into his motivations when he tells us in *The Crack-Up* that the governing principle of his earlier creative life could be summed up as: "I felt —therefore I was." He went along more or less unthinkingly (quite successful, in a material sense of the word) until he had reached the very threshold of his fortieth year. "Ten years this side of forty-nine" he suddenly cracked, suffering a breakdown of all values:

> One harassed and despairing night I packed a brief case and went off a thousand miles to think it over. I took a dollar room in a drab little town where I knew no one and sunk all the money I had with me in a stock of potted meat, crackers and apples. But don't let me suggest that the change from a rather overstuffed world to a comparative asceticism was any Research Magnificent—I only wanted absolute quiet to think out why I had developed a sad attiture toward sadness . . . *why I had become identified with the objects of my horror or compassion.*[3]

Such was the state of Fitzgerald's mind at the time he cast himself in the role of Diogenes.

It is worthwhile to note that in his critical article "How To Waste Material" written for *The Bookman* in 1926 to introduce the work of Ernest Hemingway, the one book that Fitzgerald praises most unreservedly is Cummings' autobiographical *The Enormous Room,* which was inspired by World War I. He says: "Of all the work by the young men who have sprung up since 1920 one book survives—*The Enormous Room* by E. E. Cummings. It is scarcely a novel; it doesn't deal with the American scene; it was swamped in the mediocre downpour, isolated—forgotten. But it lives on, because those few who cause books to live have not been

[3] Italics in the original.

able to endure the thought of its morality." Concerning Hemingway's *In Our Time,* which is the principal excuse for the article, he remarks that the presence of a single hero in nearly all the stories of that book causes them to take on "an almost autobiographical tint."

It is too bad that Fitzgerald was too inhibited to write more direct confessions of the kind he gave us in *The Crack-Up.* Those pieces in *Esquire* magazine were far above his usual "autobiographical" writings, such as "How To Live on $36,000 a Year," or its companion piece "How To Live on Practically Nothing a Year," or numerous others which aim at pleasant entertainment and nothing more. In *The Crack-Up* alone, one feels that the experience described was stronger than the writer. It peremptorily compelled expression and, although not quite up to the standards of Rousseau's *Confessions,* or Dostoevski's *Notes from Underground,* or Italo Svevo's *Confessions of Zeno,* its moral power is strong enough to make it an important addition not only to Fitzgerald's work but to the best American literature produced in his time.

7

THE SHORT STORIES

IN DESCRIBING the preparatory schooling of Amory Blaine in *This Side of Paradise,* Fitzgerald writes: "He read voluminously all spring, the beginning of his eighteenth year. . . . Of all his class work, only *L'Allegro* and some quality of rigid clarity in solid geometry stirred his languid interest." This "quality of rigid clarity" which Fitzgerald admired in Euclid is characteristic of his own fictional constructions but only when he is at his best. Of his novels, four out of five are deficient in some points of construction. Their plots not only lack clarity but are at times positively obscure or confused. The plots either fall into fragments without making an artistic whole, as in *This Side of Paradise* and *The Last Tycoon,* or are needlessly repetitious with an almost Dreiserian naturalism, like *The Beautiful and Damned,* or else they are split down the middle like *Tender Is the Night.* Only once did Fitzgerald make something that was aesthetically unified on a large scale, and that was *The Great Gatsby,* the book to which he will probably owe his lasting fame.

It might appear, at first thought, that the briefer compass of his short stories would make it easier for Fitzgerald to achieve the clarity and unity of construction that he so often missed or spoiled in his longer, more ambitious efforts. But it turns out, upon studying his works, that achieving an artistic unity and compactness is no easier on a small scale than on a large one. The compression of a short story's writing time into what Fitzgerald called a "hop, skip, and jump" of three days, and of the reading time into one sitting, does not itself guarantee that elusive geometrical "quality of rigid clarity" to a piece of fiction. One of Aristotle's comments in *The Poetics* on the elements of dramatic literature and their mastery might shed some light on Fitzgerald's problem:

Most important . . . is the combination of the incidents of the story. . . . One may string together a series of characteristic speeches of the utmost finish as regard Diction and Thought, and yet fail to produce the true tragic effect; but one will have much better success with a tragedy which, however inferior in these respects, has a Plot, a combination of incidents in it. . . . Beginners succeed earlier with the Diction and Characters than with the construction of a story. . . . We maintain, therefore, that the first essential, the life and soul, so to speak, of Tragedy, is the Plot, and that the Characters come second—compare the parallel in painting, where the most beautiful colors laid on without order will not give one the same pleasure as a simple black-and-white sketch of a portrait.

Fitzgerald was primarily a colorist, using the medium of words. Although we know from his correspondence with Thomas Wolfe that he aimed at mastering the architecture of literature and valued the construction of the literary form above its other qualities, it was color, nevertheless, that came easiest to him—as naturally and effortlessly as breathing itself. He is a "natural" writer, and when he was able to add the most painstaking art to his natural gifts he showed an almost unsurpassed talent for prose fiction. But Fitzgerald realized his own inadequacy in constructing logical plots, and he scolded himself for this weakness, just as he did for his other weaknesses.

There is, for example, a passage in the short story "Financing Finnegan" that refers to the "logic" of fiction. In what is admittedly a self-critical bit of slightly disguised autobiography, he says of Finnegan (who, like himself was forever living beyond his means and was consequently always on the edge of bankruptcy):

> He was the perennial man of promise in American letters—what he could actually do with words was astounding, they glowed and coruscated—he wrote sentences, paragraphs, chapters that were masterpieces of fine weaving and spinning. It was only when I met some poor devil of a screen writer who had been trying to make a logical story out of one of his books that I realized he had his enemies. . . . "It's all beautiful when you read it," this man said disgustedly, "but when your write it down plain it's like a week in the nut house."

"Writing it down plain" cuts right through the surface to the bone structure underneath. Malcolm Cowley, despite his general respect for Fitzgerald's work, finds himself in agreement with the author concerning his weak point. He says in his introduction to a selection of Fitzgerald's stories: "He never learned to be a good

95

engineer of plots." From this damaging criticism Cowley excludes only a few stories ("May Day," for instance).

The years 1925 and 1926, when the author was turning thirty, marked the high point of his creative career. One of Fitzgerald's finest stories, by general consent, is "The Rich Boy." According to Malcolm Cowley: " 'The Rich Boy' (1926) was the first serious work that Fitzgerald undertook after finishing *Gatsby*." A signal difference between these two productions deserves to be noted— his greatest novel is a masterpiece of careful plotting, while his greatest story is a masterpiece of character drawing.

From the very beginning, the writer's emphasis in this story is upon the importance of a certain kind of individuality. But it is the kind of individuality which, instead of ending in hopeless eccentricity, emerges surprisingly into the main thoroughfare of human nature. Fitzgerald is concerned here with the profound mystery explored by literature: how each man is simultaneously unique and yet basically the same as every other man; how the way to the universal leads *through* the particular rather than *around* it. Fitzgerald states the paradox near the beginning of the story: "We are all queer fish, queerer behind our faces and voices than we want any one to know or than we know ourselves. . . . There are no types, no plurals. There is a rich boy, and this is his and not his brothers' story. All my life I have lived among his brothers but this one has been my friend."

The story of Anson Hunter's life, as it unfolds, reads like the synopsis of a novel. Its length is due to the amount of time that is covered in the protagonist's life rather than to any concentration upon a particular phase of it. There are a few close-ups, particularly in the description of the hero's two love affairs and of his intervention in a relative's scandalous extramarital affair. But the story is more a *summary* of events—the type of summary that suggests the passing of years rather than any sudden illumination or depth of understanding such as might come from a less diffuse method of narration. The highest drama grows out of a severely limited plot that permits the exploration of human nature in depth. *The Great Gatsby*, for example, which covers the simple time span of one summer, contains much more dramatic power than "The Rich Boy," which covers half a lifetime. It is the interaction of half a dozen characters that gives *Gatsby* its form; "The Rich Boy" achieves its form through analysis and exposition of just one character.

What is it about Anson Hunter that Fitzgerald finally understands and is able to communicate to us? The author's most profound insight into "the rich boy" is summed up in one wonderful phrase midway in the story when he speaks of Anson as one "whose whole life was a condescension from the certitudes of his childhood." The last word serves to remind us of how carefully chosen is the word "boy" in the title. Anson's tragedy is that in some important ways he seems doomed by his wealth and the privileges it brings to perpetual immaturity. Eventually this leads him to a mild sort of breakdown or depression which renders Anson temporarily unfit, in the eyes of his business partners, to pursue his usual round of activities. They compel him to go to Europe for a vacation. In their eyes "his intense nervousness," which at another period of his life had made him so charming, had now settled into "the fussy pessimism of a man of forty."

The story ends "happily" with Anson's recovery from this depression. His buoyant spirits return, along with his confidence (which had been momentarily dampened by the feeling that life had passed him by) that "there would always be women in the world who would spend their brightest, freshest, rarest hours to nurse and protect that superiority he cherished in his heart." The narcissistic self-absorption and careless self-confidence, which in Fitzgerald's work usually characterize the beautiful and well-born girl, are here the property of a man who remains throughout his life almost half a child.

Fitzgerald was interested in laying bare the basis of the confidence possessed by Anson Hunter. In America, he thought, it could have no secure foundation except the hereditary possession of great wealth. Neither moderate wealth nor even great but uninherited wealth was sufficient to insure such confidence. A man's character is formed in childhood, and wealth therefore must be present very early in life in order to create a maximum effect upon the shaping of character. This is obviously true of Anson Hunter, who is described as "the eldest of six children who would some day divide a fortune of fifteen million dollars."

Anson's sense of superiority was nurtured from the beginning by "the half-grudging American deference that was paid to him in the Connecticut village" where the Hunter family had its summer estate. Like the mythical town of Hades in the fantasy "The Diamond as Big as the Ritz," Fitzgerald's America in general seems to be a place where "the worship of wealth is the first article of its creed."

Cowley sees in this story as well as in *Gatsby* the evidence of Fitzgerald's "complicated attitude toward the very rich, with its mixture of distrust, admiration and, above all, curiosity about how their minds work." But this admiration and even curiosity are superficial in comparison with less positive feelings aroused in him. The exposure of the cruel, seamy side of life in the Faubourg Saint-Germain by Proust has a counterpart in Fitzgerald's portrayal of the corresponding section of American society. However, the correspondence cannot be too close, since there is nothing really like a traditional aristocracy in America where traditions are still so meager and play so small a role from a practical point of view. The toleration and disinterested curiosity in Fitzgerald's narrative are intended to be characteristic of the narrator but he does not represent Fitzgerald any more closely than Gulliver represents Swift.

The fact that Anson is presented "sympathetically" to the reader makes the implied criticism of him the more damning. (It is not surprising that the man who was, apparently, the model for Fitzgerald's character was very much hurt when the story appeared, though in later years his feelings were mollified when "The Rich Boy" was recognized as one of its author's most successful creations.) The hero does not have a trace of what the narrator calls "idealism" or "illusion" in his make-up—and these qualities alone seem to make a man truly sympathetic. From the very beginning, Anson sees the world without any of the veils that usually obscure it from the eyes of the less fortunate: "Anson accepted without reservation the world of high finance and high extravagance, of divorce and dissipation, of snobbery and of privilege. Most of our lives end as a compromise—it was as a compromise that his life began."

The first (and, as it turns out, the last) really important girl in his life is Paula Legendre, who, though not as rich as Anson, is very wealthy in her own right. Their relationship, which had started well and seemed likely to end in marriage, first falters because of Anson's whimsical drinking habits. He is not a habitual drunkard, to be sure, but he drinks as the spirit moves him and, on occasion, far beyond his capacity for self-control. Although he does not indulge himself frequently—he is far too successful in business to do so—his abandon and irresponsibility alarm Paula. Yet she remains so fascinated by him that he dominated and attracted her, and at the same time filled her with anxiety. Confused by his mixture of solidity and self-indulgence, of sentiment and cynicism—incongruities which her gentle mind was unable to resolve—Paula grew to think of him as two alternating personalities. When she saw him alone, or at a formal party, as with his casual inferiors, she felt tremendous pride in his strong, attractive presence, the paternal, understanding stature of his mind. In other company she became uneasy when what had been a fine imperviousness to mere gentility showed its other face. The other face was gross, humorous, reckless of everything but pleasure. . . .

It is not necessary to detail the steps by which the relationship inevitably comes to grief. Subtly yet unmistakably, Fitzgerald succeeds in showing that the fault for this failure lies with Anson rather than Paula. His flawed integrity is too much for her relative simplicity and sincerity to overcome. All the hesitations upon the brink of marriage, to which he brings her time and again, are his fault. Anson enjoys his power over her too much to give it up voluntarily, but he will not pay the price to which his actions seem irrevocably to commit him. One day, her patience with him ends and she marries a man whom she would have willingly thrown over, if only Anson would have made up his mind to marry her. Her marriage is a terrible blow to Anson's pride: "One thing he could not help—for three days, in any place, in any company, he would suddenly bend his head into his hands and cry like a child." The childishness of one side of Anson Hunter's nature resounds like a leitmotiv throughout the story.

Paula's importance in Anson's life, however, does not end with her marriage. Several years later, she divorces Lowell Thayer of Boston, and then remarries. When Anson accidentally encounters her, she is pregnant. She is glad to see him, and he goes to visit her and her new husband, Peter Hagerty. Anson is convinced by what ensues that she has gotten over her disappointment in him. She tells him quite unaffectedly that she is in love for the first time with her new husband. Her feeling for Anson, she now says, had been mere infatuation. She tells him: "You could make me do anything you liked. But we wouldn't have been happy. I'm not smart enough for you. I don't like things to be complicated like you do. You'll never settle down."

It is after this chance meeting with Paula that Anson comes close to losing his nerve. He is then pressed by his business associates to take a trip abroad in an effort to restore his morale. What restores it, however, is not the trip itself but the news, which reaches him three days before sailing, that Paula had died in childbirth! He shows not the slightest tremor of remorse or regret for her unhappy fate. The narrator informs us that "for the first time in our friendship he told me not a word of how he felt, nor did I see the slightest sign of emotion. His chief preoccupation was with the fact that he was thirty years old. . . ." He at once embarks on a new affair with a girl whom he meets on board ship, and he tells the narrator his romantic adventures with his old, familiar gusto "making them all bizarre and amusing, as he had a way of doing." The narrator's dry comment on all this is simply: "I was glad that he was himself again, or at least the self that I knew, and with which I felt at home."

Such is an outline of the main events of the story, but its moral is reinforced by two other episodes that take place—Anson's relation with a girl named Dolly Karger, and the relation between him and his uncle, Robert Hunter. Dolly Karger is a rather "fast" New York society girl, of doubtful antecedents. Anson meets her less than a month after Paula's first marriage and begins a flighty affair: "He was drinking rather heavily, and he pretended for a week that he was falling in love with her. Then he dropped her abruptly and forgot—immediately he took up the commanding position in her heart." (The seesaw rhythm of love is familiar to all readers of Stendhal and Proust, and we are not surprised to hear that Fitzgerald was a confirmed Proustian and actively proselytized among his most intimate friends to get them to appreciate, if they did not already do so, *A la recherche du temps perdu*.)

Thus far in the affair, Anson's relation to Dolly is perfectly understandable and, by the lax standards of his time and place, defensible, but what follows is much less so. The trouble begins with an episode that Fitzgerald seems to have fashioned closely upon a Proustian model. Anson writes a farewell letter to Dolly, but as he steps outside his house to mail it, he meets the postman bringing him a letter from her instead—"a short, somewhat formal note" in which she tells him that she will be unable to go to the country with him that weekend because of the unexpected arrival in town of Perry Hull, a friend of hers from Chicago.

The letter describes Perry as "*so* nice, and he so much wants to marry me. . . ." Though Anson sees through Dolly's "pathetic ruse" immediately, he is unable to resist allowing this new element in the situation to influence his behavior: "He was not jealous—she meant nothing to him—but . . . everything stubborn and self-indulgent in him came to the surface." And so he is moved to exercise the "power of fascination" that he feels he has over her. He tears up his own letter to her, calls on her in spite of her protest that she has another date, and quickly convinces her that he is still the master of her heart. He takes her to an estate in Port Washington where he is determined to complete his seduction of her. At the last moment, however, he stops himself, confessing that he does not love her, never has loved her, and is acting simply out of pique. As he leaves her room, his cousin unexpectedly returns to the deserted house. "For a long time afterward Anson believed that a protective God sometimes interfered in human affairs. But Dolly Karger, lying awake and staring at the ceiling, never again believed in anything at all."

Anson, we are convinced then, is a very lucky fellow but not a sensitive or particularly scrupulous one. This same quality of thick-skinned, self-centered egotism is revealed in an even more glaring light in his relations with his uncle, Robert Hunter. Anson learns from town gossip (which is often the way Fitzgerald's characters receive important news) that his Aunt Edna is carrying on a clandestine affair with a certain "dissolute, hard-drinking young man named Cary Sloane." Anson's family pride is hurt by the whispers that he hears, and while his uncle is vacationing at Hot Springs, he makes an appointment with his aunt and accuses her with brutal directness of betraying her husband. She resists the accusation for a time, but his pertinacity beats down her defences at last. The next step obviously is to have Cary Sloane present at their confrontation, and it is hardly a surprise that he proves no match for the determined, self-confident Anson. In the course of their bitter exchanges, Anson tells Sloane the right by which he has taken it upon himself to intervene: "Why—she owes this house and the rings on her fingers to my father's brains. When Uncle Robert married her she didn't have a penny." He then threatens the guilty, cowering couple that if they do not follow his orders, he will go first to his Uncle Robert with the whole story and afterward to the young man's father, Moses Sloane.

They capitulate, and he tells them his terms: Cary Sloane must leave town within forty-eight hours and stay away for at least six months; when he gets back there must be no resumption of the illicit relationship, but "at the end of a year Edna might, if she wished, tell Robert Hunter that she wanted a divorce and go about it in the usual way." They agree to his demands—there is nothing else for them to do—and Anson departs from the scene with a feeling of self-satisfaction: "This was his city, he thought, where his name had flourished through five generations."

Before morning, Cary Sloane has killed himself by plunging from a high bridge, but "Anson never blamed himself for his part in this affair —the situation which brought it about had not been of his making. But the just suffer with the unjust, and he found that his oldest and somehow his most precious friendship was over. He never knew what distorted story Edna told, but he was welcome in his uncle's house no longer." The irony (which Fitzgerald himself in *The Beautiful and Damned* had called "the Holy Ghost of this latter day") with which the author salts such a passage is so slight as to be almost imperceptible, yet it is unmistakably present in words like "the just suffer with the unjust." This particular episode (which has overtones not unlike some of those heard in *The Great Gatsby* during the confrontation of Tom Buchanan and his rival in a room of the Plaza hotel in New York —with Anson here playing a somewhat similar role to that of Tom in the earlier work) makes one aware that Fitzgerald's exposure of the savagery found in even the most rarefied circles of our civilization is sometimes characterized by truly profound satiric indignation.

Behind the glittering façade of wit, fashion, and superficial friendliness, Anson Hunter exhibits a cold indifference to the feelings of everyone but himself. Through the gloss of surface charm, a fundamental failure in human sympathy becomes clearly visible. It is in the light of this exposure that we must read Fitzgerald's oft-quoted but misunderstood passage from "The Rich Boy": "Let me tell you about the very rich. They are different from you and me. . . . Even when they enter deep into our world or sink below us, they still think that they are better than we are. They are different. . . ."

The same theme appears in inverted form in the famous story "Winter Dreams," which might just as appropriately have been called "The Rich Girl" since it is concerned with the pathetic frustration of Dexter Green (who plays the role of Paula here and whose name, significantly, indicates his stage of spiritual development—the time before his youthful illusions have worn off). The cause of Dexter's unhappiness is Judy Jones, who belongs, beneath her commonplace name, to the same species as Anson Hunter and

Daisy Buchanan. Certain descriptions of all three characters appear to be almost interchangeable—it is not Judy alone who is characterized in the following sentences: "She was entertained only by the gratification of her desires and by the direct exercise of her own charm. Perhaps from so much youthful love, so many youthful lovers, she had come, in self-defense, to nourish herself wholly from within."

The very rich, in Fitzgerald's stories, are not particularly happy in their opportunities to indulge their whims. Judy Jones ends in "Winter Dreams" as a faded beauty and a maltreated wife, just as Daisy Buchanan had ended in *The Great Gatsby*. Anson Hunter in "The Rich Boy" is no exception; at the conclusion of the story we see him as a disgruntled, aging bachelor, envying his married friends and deriving a niggardly pleasure from the misfortunes that overtake them. He is still engaged in pursuing girls, but with diminishing conviction that they have any stable happiness to bring him. He is still the rich "boy" who, as Paula had prophesied, will never consent to the necessity of becoming mature.

"The life of the poor," however, as Fitzgerald calls it in his story "The Sensible Thing," is ever more bitter. There is no fun for George O'Kelly in being "an insurance clerk at forty dollars a week with his dream slipping fast behind him." One of Fitzgerald's fictional "tricks" is to allow his hero a sudden social rise and then to see what difference this will make in him. In a brief period of time, George O'Kelly "had risen from poverty into a position of unlimited opportunity." And, of course, social values being what they are in the world he inhabits, the girl and everything else in life that had hitherto proved so elusive to his grasp, now yield somewhat hurriedly to him. Over and over again, the same note is sounded in Fitzgerald's stories. In "May Day," Edith rejects Gordon Sterrett when he tells her that he has failed and is "poor as hell." Though she has just been thinking of him with the most romantic tenderness, his pessimistic words destroy in a single moment all her enthusiasm for him. In "The Last of the Belles," Lieutenant Earl Schoen finds himself rebuffed by the Southern heroine because, as soon as he is separated from the glamor of his wartime uniform, he proves to be nothing but a street-car conductor with no suitable "background" at all. In "The Freshest Boy," the romantic captain of the Yale football team, Ted Fay, is compelled to learn the economic facts of life from a showgirl, who has irrevocably committed her future to a Mr. Beltzman, the backer of the musical comedy in which she is playing. The scene in which she tells him the brutal truth is seen through the eyes of the boy Basil who becomes aware, almost as a Dreiserian hero might, that "life for everybody was a struggle, sometimes magnificent from a distance, but always difficult and surprisingly simple and a little sad."

Only in "The Bridal Party" is the notion of the all-powerful role of wealth in America challenged. The hero of the story, Michael Curly, consoles himself for losing his favorite girl with the reflection that it could hardly have been otherwise, since he has no money and "Caroline had lost faith and begun to see him as something pathetic, futile and shabby, outside the great, shining stream of life toward which she was inevitably drawn." But then, in Fitzgerald's usual fashion, an almost magical reversal makes Michael the unexpected heir of a quarter of a million dollars. By coincidence, his successful rival in love, on the very eve of his marriage, has lost all his money in the stock market. Yet, these developments make surprisingly little difference to the heroine, who still chooses the same bridegroom she has chosen before. Although Fitzgerald seems to be suggesting here that some of the old-fashioned virtues are more important than the number of integers in one's bank balance, his message actually is the same as it had been all along. The world he describes belongs to those who are strong enough to take it. Michael Curly, in spite of his inherited wealth, is really a weak character who has had some luck, while his successful rival is one of the masterful men in his society—like Dreiser's Frank Cowperwood, for example—whether or not he has money at the moment. He is one of those men who may be "broke" but who can never be poor (because the latter, in contrast to the former, is not so much a physical as a psychological state). Hamilton Rutherford has a solid basis of character for his confidence, not merely accidental good fortune. He goes through with his wedding in the grand style in which it had been planned, because he is sure that though he is ruined temporarily, he will be back at the top of his world very soon. One of the wedding guests sums up the moral of all this in the comment: "It's amazing. This show will cost him about five thousand dollars, and I understand they'll be just about his last. But did he countermand a bottle of champagne or a flower? Not he! He happens to have it—that young man. Do you know that T. G. Vance offered him a salary of fifty thousand dollars a year ten minutes before the wedding this morning? In another year he'll be back with the millionaires."

Thus, money itself is not as important as the confidence that usually (but not always) goes with money. The rewards go to the confident men, since it is natural for them sooner or later to command money. Tragedy results when, as in the case of Gordon Sterrett in "May Day," the confidence of a man cracks under the pressure of financial insolvency. The Hamilton Rutherfords of Fitzgerald's world never have to fear this. There is an energy and will about them that no mere monetary crack-up can destroy. This modification, which had been introduced earlier by Dreiser in his treatment of the career of the financier Cowperwood, is the only one that Fitzgerald is willing to make in his definition of the meaning of success in American terms. Properly understood, such a modification strengthens rather than weakens the author's thesis that a ruthless, materialistic standard of values has the best chance of prevailing in the context of contemporary American civilization. The more dispirited forebodings of Whitman in *Democratic Vistas* concerning the future development of American materialism (forebodings which he shared with other later nineteenth-century writers as different from each other as Henry Adams and Mark Twain) were destined to be realized during the first three decades of the twentieth century which form the social background for most of Fitzgerald's stories.

The one quality of Fitzgerald's stories that, somehow, even those with a taste for his best works do not mention is the sheer delight that his romantic fantasies and humorous anecdotes bring, even when their subject matter is seemingly most trivial and ephemeral. In *The Moveable Feast,* Hemingway says that when he first met Fitzgerald, he thought of him as a popular writer for *The Saturday Evening Post,* who was capable of producing stories that were always quite readable but certainly not "serious," since they did not leave any residue of thought behind in the reader's mind. Although that is not precisely how he puts it, it is essentially what he means. It is hardly necessary to say that academic readers and critics have formed no kinder opinion of this part of Fitzgerald's *oeuvre* than did Hemingway.

Dare one suggest that they may be wrong? It is far from our intention to deny the distinction that Whitman implies in *Democratic Vistas* when he speaks of a nation that possesses "rivers and oceans of very readable print" but has no literature at all in the proper sense of the word. What we affirm is that Fitzgerald's less celebrated "potboiling" creations have a quality in our eyes which brings them into the category of literature. To be specific, a story such as "The Offshore Pirate," from his early collection *Flappers and Philosophers,* despite the fact that it has no memorable meaning or message and is therefore either unnoticed or despised by most readers, is so delightful and dreamlike a fantasy that it stands no more in need of intellectual justification than a beautiful piece of music or certain lyric poems. In a well-known formulation, Archibald MacLeish affirms that "a poem should not mean, but be." But no one seems to have noticed that stories in prose have the same license. Fitzgerald's story corresponds to its author's daydreams; it is built out of airy wish-fulfillments; as such, it will strike a responsive chord in its readers. In any case, a creation which, after more than forty years, still retains a feeling of freshness and surprise cannot be shrugged off as a "readable" magazine piece. Whether or not we can explain its effect, is it not characteristic of "news that stays news" (as literature has been defined by Pound) to retain precisely the impression of freshness and charm which even Fitzgerald's most trivial stories make upon us to this day? Equally delightful are Fitzgerald's humorous anecdotes like "The Camel's Back." This, too, makes no pretense to "deep" meanings or satiric overtones of an intellectual kind. But it seems as assured of permanence as any of the more self-consciously "serious" literary efforts of our time because it will cause hilarity in this or any century. Our concept of literature, then, may require some rethinking and broadening to include such efforts.

Some of Fitzgerald's fantasies, of course, do have "deeper" meanings and broader satirical intentions of a more social kind. This is true of his generally admired story "The Diamond as Big as the Ritz." Such works need no defense, of course, but they seem to be no finer aesthetically than more "purposeless" creations. Consider one of his humorous fantasies: "The Case of Benjamin Button." The "idea" here is a very simple one—to have a man who is born old regress with the passage of time until he reaches childhood and infancy. It is carried out beautifully, logically, and with the most lively inventiveness. Turning time upside down in this way is not only amusing in its consequences but revealing and instructive in many respects as well. In fact, what began as a wild fantasy ends almost on a note of realism, for in the ordinary course of things old age paradoxically reaches the stage of "second childhood" also.

No one has ever made any great claims for the "seriousness" of "The Case of Benjamin Button" or its pre-eminence in any other way. It represents the average of what Fitzgerald was capable of achieving in his lightest moods; what a high average it turns out to be!

8

CONCLUSION:

THE POET FITZGERALD

THE WORD POET is used by Aristotle and the Greeks to mean "maker," and when we inquire as to what it is that the poet *makes,* we discover that he is the maker of outlines—plots—of stories. The management of these plots, or story lines (which, as noted earlier, Aristotle compares to line drawings of portraits) is, according to the *Poetics,* the first and most important element of both the drama and the epic. The creation of character is subordinate to it, as are diction, style, thought, and the mastery of words and phrases, all of which are still lower on the list. Included in the latter is the creation of various figures of speech, of which metaphor is the most important. Metaphor, Aristotle indicates categorically, is the hallmark of genius. Its richness depends on a certain keenness of perception, an ability to see resemblances between things which superficially do not seem to have much in common.

The several millennia that have elapsed since Aristotle's time have made a difference in our use of words. The word poet has become much more specialized in its meaning. Today it has little to do with the making of plot outlines or the creation of character; it has everything to do with the handling of words in a special way. This latter idea probably owes its origin to the movement called romanticism. One of the most important early forerunners of romanticism was the German writer Johann von Herder, who, in a memorable sentence says: "The essence of poetry is the power that cleaves to words, a magic power that works upon my soul through fantasy and recollection."

Today the use of the word "poetry" is generally much closer to Herder's conception of it than to Aristotle's. It could certainly be argued that Fitzgerald was a poet in the Aristotelian sense of the term. His handling of the plot in *Gatsby,* for instance, is excellent, and the pacing of the scenes which lead up to the death of Mildred Wilson and its tragic consequences has something of the magnitude —grandeur even—and chilling sense of inevitability that one associates with the Greek drama. But when we speak of Fitzgerald as a poet it is not usually in this sense. What we mean is Fitzgerald, the marvelous verbal choreographer and coiner of images which have lost none of their minted freshness after almost half a century. And it is in Fitzgerald's prose that his poetry appears. In this respect he resembles earlier American writers such as Melville.

Whereas Melville's literary models were Milton, Shakespeare, and the Elizabethans, Fitzgerald's descriptions in this and other books recall the effects achieved by the poet Keats. In a passage from *The Crack-Up* (the letters to his daughter) which was referred to in the introduction, Fitzgerald makes a confession of taste that is vital to an understanding of his own style:

> "The Grecian Urn" is unbearably beautiful, with every syllable as inevitable as the notes in Beethoven's Ninth Symphony, or it's something you don't understand. It is what it is because an extraordinary genius paused at that point in history and touched it. . . . Likewise . . . the "Nightingale," which I can never read through without tears in my eyes; likewise the "Pot of Basil" with its great stanzas about the two brothers "Why were they proud, etc." and "The Eve of Saint Agnes" which has the richest, most sensuous imagery in English, not excepting Shakespeare. And finally his three or four great sonnets: "Bright Star" and the others. . . . Knowing those things very young and granted an ear, one could scarcely ever afterwards be unable to distinguish between gold and dross in what one read. In themselves those eight poems are a scale of workmanship for anybody who wants to know truly about words, their most utter value for evocation, persuasion, charm. For awhile after you quit Keats all other poetry seems to be only whistling or humming.

Using this passage as a clue, let us compare Keats's "Isabella" or "The Pot of Basil" with Fitzgerald's *Tender Is the Night*. Two stanzas in "Isabella" sound oddly familiar to the reader who remembers his Fitzgerald in detail. Keats writes:

> With her two brothers this fair lady dwelt,
> Enrichèd from ancestral merchandize,
> And for them many a weary hand did swelt
> In torchèd mines and noisy factories . . .

109

> For them the Ceylon diver held his breath,
> And went all naked to the hungry shark;
> For them his ears gush'd blood; for them in death
> The seal on the cold ice with piteous bark
> Lay full of darts; for them alone did seethe
> A thousand men in troubles wide and dark:
> Half-ignorant, they turn'd an easy wheel,
> That set sharp racks at work, to pinch and peel.

The ear attuned to Fitzgerald recognizes the origin here of the well-known satiric description of the heroine of *Tender Is the Night*:

Nicole was the product of much ingenuity and toil. For her sake trains began their run at Chicago and traversed the round belly of the continent to California; chicle factories fumed and link belts grew link by link in factories; men mixed toothpaste in vats and drew mouthwash out of copper hogsheads; girls canned tomatoes quickly in August or worked rudely at the five-and-tens on Christmas Eve; half-breed Indians toiled on Brazilian coffee plantations and dreamers were muscled out of patent rights in new tractors—these were some of the people who gave a tithe to Nicole. . . .

Malcolm Cowley quotes this passage in a discussion of the social conscience of Fitzgerald, but it would seem to be as relevant to an examination of the literary influences upon him. If a social conscience is at all involved here, it appears to be something he had assimilated sympathetically along with much else from the poetry of Keats. The resemblances between his work and that of the English poet, of course, are not always so obvious or direct. In a passage from *Gatsby*, they are much more subtly evident:

A breeze blew through the room, blew curtains in at one end and out the other like pale flags, twisting them toward the frosted wedding-cake of the ceiling, and then rippled over the wine-colored rug, making a shadow on it as the wind does on the sea. The only completely stationary object in the room was an enormous couch on which two young women were buoyed up as though upon an anchored balloon. They were both in white, and their dresses were rippling and fluttering as if they had just been blown back in after a short flight around the house.

Proust has some interesting thoughts on the nature of metaphor which, like Aristotle, he regards as a most important index of the quality of a writer's talent. He thinks that metaphors (like an impressionist painter's use of colors) originate in a writer's untutored sense-impressions, before the intervention of critical intellect. It is very different from the faculty that leads to orderly abstract generalizations. At their best, metaphors are stamped with a truth of their own which is found in all powerful first impressions, however defiant of reason they seem. This meaning may be illustrated by metaphors which Fitzgerald, finding no use for them in his works, carefully hoarded for future use in his notebooks. We find, for example, Fitzgerald speaking of "the nineteen wild green eyes of a bus [which] were coming up to them in the dark." And, again, of "a sound of clinking waiters." Everyone, with a little reflection, will recognize the basis of these happy comparisons, which come through to us almost as if they were a personal remembrance. Somewhere, sometime we ourselves have seen those nineteen wild green eyes of the bus. And how many times have we heard the sound of a waiter before catching sight of him?

Fitzgerald had the ability to seize hold of a fleeting moment and to convey its impact without waiting for the intervention of reason to remove the rawness of reality. The poet's brilliance often dazzles us even before we fully understand his meaning, and perhaps this reaction corresponds to the order of his own experience; the electrifying image has, perhaps, taken him by surprise before he has grasped it intellectually. It may be a similar desire for the immediate impression in literature that lies at the bottom of Aristotle's well-known recommendation to the dramatist that he should begin his story's action in the midst of things. In other words, he should be concerned with arresting our attention even at the cost of a story's purely logical development which would require him to go back at once to its true beginning. Let him start at a point of great intensity instead and then work backward to straighten out things as a flashback in a movie does with an exposition of the necessary facts in order to understand the story fully. This seems to indicate that the writer must engage the feelings of his audience before he appeals to its mind. If the most intellectual of critics is aware of this truth, Fitzgerald never forgets it.

It is possible to imagine Fitzgerald crying out, like Keats, for a life of sensations rather than thoughts. However, both are thinkers, too, almost in spite of themselves, and one can trace the deep moral and philosophical foundations beneath their work which help to sustain their art. But we are concerned here with the outermost layer of charm and beauty in the texture of Fitzgerald's prose, which stems from his ability to create an illusion based on the true order in which rapidly flitting impressions actually come to us. Consider, for example, this lovely sentence from *Gatsby*: "The lawn started at the beach and ran toward the front door for a quarter of a mile, jumping over sundials and brick walls and burning gardens—finally when it reached the house drifting up the side in bright vines as though from the momentum of its run." The author himself may have been astonished at the remarkable conclusion of this sentence. Much that has been said here about literature in general and metaphor in particular seems to have been said already by Robert Frost in his characteristically laconic way: "The logic is backward, in retrospect, after the act. It must be more felt than seen ahead like prophecy. It must be a revelation, or series of revelations, as much for the poet as for the reader." Or, to put it in other words by Frost: "No surprise for the writer, no surprise for the reader." In Fitzgerald, the order is always determined by actual perception rather than by intellectual reconstruction. He catches his impressions on the wing as it were; he does not permit them to become abstractions. That is why such a description as this one from "Babylon Revisited" refuses to fade in color after more than a generation: "The Place de la Concorde moved by in pink majesty; they crossed the logical Seine, and Charlie felt the sudden provincial quality of the left bank."

Fitzgerald's eye for resemblances can unexpectedly link together the most distant parts of human experience so that the effect of his similes, precisely because of their accuracy, is often extremely droll. Thus, in his story "May Day" he speaks of a room which "seemed to empty like a wash bowl." In "Crazy Sunday," the Great Lover of the screen watches the poor protagonist making a fool of himself "with an eye as keen as the eye of a potato." No less apt (though less humorous) is his description of the heroine of the story: "There she was, in a dress like ice-water, made in a thousand pale-blue pieces, with icicles at the throat."

It is clear from Fitzgerald's notebooks that these remarkably striking comparisons were created with the greatest of care. They may be inspired but in most cases they were not improvised on the spur of the moment and the impression of spontaneity which they produce turns out to be a carefully calculated effect. Fitzgerald notebooks were for him a sort of bank where he deposited, day by day, the observations and figures of speech for which he had no immediate use but which, when called upon, served him as the most ornamental and even integral features of his finished work. This conclusion is prompted by an entry in *The Crack-Up:* "Learning of a word or place etc., and then seeming to run across the word or place in your reading constantly in the next few weeks. Use as simile: 'as when on' etc." His economical use of images is a vital element in the poetic brilliance and imaginative luster of the final product of his creative activity.

The high polish of Fitzgerald's art is often the result, as it is with other famous writers, of a matchless capacity for taking pains. He is capable, like Proust, of renewing our awareness of the most familiar and commonplace experiences. Proust writes of an old man's wrinkled hands "as if they had been left lying too long in water," and Fitzgerald describes a winter's day in his sentence: "It was late February and an eager, unpunctilious sun was turning the scrawny street snow into dirty cheerful rivulets that echoes in the gutters." Occasionally though, Fitzgerald seems to push a little too hard to achieve a feeling of originality. He is capable of basing a metaphor on a mere play of words, as when he speaks of "a trolley running on the crack of dawn," or when he describes "a toiling sweating sun [that] stoked the sky overhead." He has the defects of his virtues.

In his best descriptions, however, Fitzgerald's wit combines with his metaphor: "She was a stalk of ripe corn, but bound not as cereals are but as a rare first edition, with all the binder's art. She was lovely and expensive and about nineteen." The cynicism here is reminiscent of Gatsby when he describes Daisy's voice as being "full of . . . money." Such an image bears the same mark of permanence as some of Flaubert's images do in *Madame Bovary*: "Charles's conversation was commonplace as a street pavement . . ."; or the description of the cap which Charles wore as a schoolboy: "one of those head-gears of composite order, in which we can find traces of the bearskin, shako, billycock hat, sealskin cap, and cotton nightcap; *one of those poor things, in short, the dumb ugliness of which has depths of expression, like an imbecile's face.*" [1] Flaubert spoke of the *mot juste*, which the writer's researches were designed to discover, but it is not so much the single word that is important as the *cluster* of words that go into the metaphor or simile and that light up the page so brilliantly.

---

[1] Italics added by author.

Style in a writer is an elusive subject. Fitzgerald himself was inclined to scoff when an explanation of it was attempted on an academic level. To his daughter at Vassar when she proposed taking a course in modern English prose, he wrote sarcastically: "I don't care how clever the professor is, one can't raise a discussion of modern prose above a tea-table level." Nevertheless, he tried to pass on to her some of the secrets of style he had learned the hard way through long practice: "A good style simply doesn't *form* unless you absorb half a dozen top-flight authors every year. Or rather it forms, but instead of being a subconscious amalgam of all that you have admired, it is simply a reflection of the last writer you have read, a watered-down journalese." In his notebooks, meant for his own use, he sometimes made remarks on the subject which were more cryptic: "The queer slanting effect of the substantive, the future imperfect, a matter of intuition or ear to O'Hara, is unknown to careful writers like Bunny and John." Style to him seems to be something which is created below the level of consciousness to be appreciated by intuition rather than by analysis. Notable intellectuals like his friends Edmund Wilson and John Peale Bishop, to whom he refers, are less apt to master its mysteries than a man like John O'Hara who relies on his literary instincts and feelings.

If Fitzgerald's work increasingly detaches itself from its time, the reason must be sought first of all in his style. The sensitive reader could recognize his hand even if the work were anonymous. Who else would think of describing a girl who *"melted* into the color of the room"? Who would write of "metropolitan days and nights that were tense as singing wires"? The aesthetic sensitivity which produced such similes may serve as a touchstone for what is most valuable in the whole field of modern American literature. The volume of his best works, like that of Keats, may be slight, but the proportion of gold in it is relatively high.

The influence of Fitzgerald's style upon his contemporaries and his successors is obviously much less than that of his friend Hemingway. Hemingway's style swept all before it for a time. It was the very stuff that fashions and feverish enthusiasms are made of, and fortunately it was simple enough (at least on the surface) to be successfully copied by those who were struck by its charms. Fitzgerald's felicities, on the other hand, are much more subtle, and his effects are more complex and difficult to recapture. One can easily imitate Hemingway's mannerisms, but to copy Fitzgerald's manner really requires close study if one is going to try to compete with it at all.

114

Henry Dan Piper, in his book on Fitzgerald, thinks he can detect Fitzgerald's influence in the work of William Styron and perhaps J. D. Salinger as well. A much more striking example of his stylistic influence can be found in the writings of Philip Roth. There are lengthy passages in *Goodbye, Columbus,* which a good reader quite possibly could mistake for the prose of Fitzgerald. Roth displays a mockingbird's gift for mimicking the very intonations of Fitzgerald, who supplies him with both his subject (the poor boy on the make in America, whose affair with a girl richer than himself is socially doomed from the beginning, though neither of them knows it) as well as with the sentence rhythms with which to tell the story.

But *influence* is not necessarily related to the *importance* of a writer. Many of those capable of creating fashions have very little lasting value as far as art is concerned. The greatest writers have not been the most influential, or at least their influence is not easily discerned. They create a certain atmosphere to which writers in the future respond without necessarily realizing it. In fact, the very excellence of certain writers discourages others from imitating them and therefore reduces their influence. Lesser writers are often much more effective style setters precisely because they are more "imitable." The direct influence of Keats upon certain poems of Matthew Arnold is clearly traceable, but his indirect influence upon many others is more important. Among the romantics, it was Byron's style that was generally imitated, just as among twentieth-century writers Hemingway was copied, and for the same reason perhaps— they were both "catchy" and simple enough to invite emulation. Of all the writers in the English language, Shakespeare has perhaps the least discernible influence, unless one agrees, as one should, that he has influenced all those who wrote in the English language after him and that his influence has been so diffuse and generalized that writers imitate Shakespeare unconsciously.

It is thoughts like this that may have prompted the tribute to Fitzgerald from his Princeton teacher and friend, Christian Gauss, with whom he maintained a lifelong relationship. In a letter of congratulations on the publication of *Tender Is the Night,* Gauss wrote him:

Without any disrespect to him I put Hemingway down at the infrared side and you on the ultraviolet. His rhythm is like the beating of an African tom-tom—primitive, simple, but it gets you in the end. . . . You are on the other end. You have a feeling for musical

(115)

intervals and the tone-color of words which makes your prose the finest instrument for rendering all the varied shades of our complex emotional states. There are passages that I read over and over to myself as I would read a poem.

That is the tribute of a very good reader to an excellent writer, and it sums up the case on F. Scott Fitzgerald's behalf as well as he or anyone who has ever admired his work could wish.

SELECTED BIBLIOGRAPHY

Barrett, William. "Fitzgerald and America," *Partisan Review,* XVIII (May–June 1951).

Beebe, Maurice, and Jackson R. Bryer. "Criticism of F. Scott Fitzgerald: A Selected Checklist," *Modern Fiction Studies,* VII (Spring 1961), 82–94.

Bewley, Marius. "Scott Fitzgerald and the Collapse of the American Dream," in *The Eccentric Design.* New York: Columbia University Press, 1959.

Bishop, John Peale. "The Missing All," *The Virginia Quarterly Review,* XIII (Winter 1937).

Brucolli, Matthew. *The Composition of* Tender Is the Night: *A Study of the Manuscripts.* Pittsburgh: Pittsburgh University Press.

Bryer, Jackson R. "F. Scott Fitzgerald and His Critics: A Bibliographical Record," *Bulletin of Bibliography,* XXIII (1962), 155–158, 180–183, 201–208.

———. "F. Scott Fitzgerald: A Review of Research and Scholarship," *Texas Studies in Literature and Language,* V (Spring 1963), 147–163.

Cowley, Malcolm. "Fitzgerald: The Double Man," *Saturday Review,* XXXIV (February 24, 1951).

———. "F. Scott Fitzgerald: The Romance of Money," *The Western Review,* XVII (Summer 1953), 245–255.

———, ed. *The Stories of F. Scott Fitzgerald.* New York: Charles Scribner's Sons, 1951.

———, ed. *Three Novels of F. Scott Fitzgerald.* New York: Charles Scribner's Sons, 1953.

Eble, Kenneth. *F. Scott Fitzgerald.* New York: Twayne Publishers, Inc., 1963.

Fitzgerald, Zelda. *Save Me the Waltz.* New York: Charles Scribner's Sons, 1953; and London: Grey Wales Press, 1953.

Frohock, W. M. "Morals, Manners, and S. Fitzgerald," *The Southwest Review,* XL (Summer 1958), 220–228.

Geismar, Maxwell. "F. Scott Fitzgerald: Orestes at the Ritz," *The Last of the Provincials: The American Novel 1915–1925.* Boston: Houghton, Mifflin Co., 1943.

Goldhurst, William. *F. Scott Fitzgerald and His Contemporaries.* Cleveland: World Publishing Company, 1963.

Graham, Sheilah, and Gerold Frank. *Beloved Infidel*. New York: Holt, Rinehart and Winston, Inc., 1958.

Gringrich, Arnold, ed. *The Pat Hobby Stories*. New York: Charles Scribner's Sons, 1962.

Hemingway, Ernest. *A Moveable Feast*. New York: Charles Scribner's Sons, 1964.

Hindus, Milton. "F. Scott Fitzgerald and Fashionable Literary Anti-Semitism," *Commentary* (June 1947).

———. "The Mysterious Eye of Dr. T. J. Eckleburg," *Boston University Studies in English,* III (Spring 1957), 22–31.

———. "The Great Fitzgerald," *The New Leader* (May 19, 1958).

———. "Disintegrating Genius," *The New Leader* (February 16, 1959), 22–23.

Hoffman, Frederick J. *The Great Gatsby: A Study*. New York: Charles Scribner's Sons, 1962.

Kazin, Alfred. *F. Scott Fitzgerald: The Man and His Work* (a collection of critical articles by various people). Cleveland: World Publishing Company, 1952.

Kuehl, John, ed. *The Apprentice Fiction of F. Scott Fitzgerald*. New Brunswick, N.J.: Rutgers University Press, 1965.

Lehan, Richard D. *F. Scott Fitzgerald*. Carbondale, Illinois: Southern Illinois University Press, 1966.

Mackendrick, Paul. *"The Great Gatsby* and Trimalchio," *The Classical Journal,* XLV (April 1950), 307–315.

Miller, James E. *F. Scott Fitzgerald: His Art and Technique*. New York: New York University Press, 1964.

Mizener, Arthur. *The Far Side of Paradise*. Boston: Houghton, Mifflin Co., 1951.

———, ed. *Afternoon of an Author*. Princeton, N.J.: Princeton University Library, 1958.

———. *F. Scott Fitzgerald: A Collection of Critical Articles*. Englewood Cliffs, N.J.: Prentice-Hall, Inc., 1963.

Morris, Wright. "The Ability to Function. A Reappraisal of Fitzgerald and Hemingway," *New World Writing,* No. 13. New York, 1958.

Perosa, Sergio. *The Art of F. Scott Fitzgerald*. Ann Arbor, Mich.: The University of Michigan Press, 1965.

Piper, Henry Dan. *F. Scott Fitzgerald: A Critical Portrait*. New York: Holt, Rinehart and Winston, Inc., 1965.

Ralegh, John H. *"The Great Gatsby*: Legendary Basis and Allegorical Significance," The University of Kansas City Review, XXIV (October 1957), 55–58.

Shain, Charles E. *F. Scott Fitzgerald*. Minneapolis: The University of Minnesota Press, 1961.

Shulberg, Budd. "Old Scott: The Mask, the Myth, and the Man," *Esquire*, LV (January 1961).

Stallman, Robert W. "Conrad and *The Great Gatsby*," *Twentieth Century Literature*, I (April 1955).

Taylor, Dwight. "S. Fitzgerald in Hollywood," *Harper's* (March 1959).

Trilling, Lionel. Introduction to *The Great Gatsby*. New York: Charles Scribner's Sons, 1945.

Troy, William. "Scott Fitzgerald—The Authority of Failure," *Accent*, 1945.

Turnbull, Andrew. *Scott Fitzgerald*. New York: Charles Scribner's Sons, 1962.

———. *The Letters of F. Scott Fitzgerald*. New York: Charles Scribner's Sons, 1963.

Wilson, Edmund. "Imaginary Conversations: Mr. V. W. Brooks and Mr. S. Fitzgerald," *The New Republic*, XXXIII (April 30, 1924), 249–254.

———, ed. Scott Fitzgerald's *The Last Tycoon*. New York: Charles Scribner's Sons, 1941.

———, ed. Scott Fitzgerald's *The Crack-Up*. New York: New Directions, 1945.

WORKS OF F. SCOTT FITZGERALD

This Side of Paradise. New York: Charles Scribner's Sons, 1920.

Flappers and Philosophers. New York: Charles Scribner's Sons, 1920.

The Beautiful and Damned. New York: Charles Scribner's Sons, 1922.

Tales of the Jazz Age. New York: Charles Scribner's Sons, 1922.

The Vegetable. New York: Charles Scribner's Sons, 1923.

The Great Gatsby. New York: Charles Scribner's Sons, 1925.

All the Sad Young Men. New York: Charles Scribner's Sons, 1926.

Tender Is the Night. New York: Charles Scribner's Sons, 1934.

Taps at Reveille. New York: Charles Scribner's Sons, 1935.

The Last Tycoon. New York: Charles Scribner's Sons, 1941.

The Crack-Up. New York: New Directions, 1945.

Afternoon of an Author. Princeton, N.J.: Princeton University Library, 1958.

The Pat Hobby Stories. New York: Charles Scribner's Sons, 1962.

INDEX

INDEX

Note: Characters and other fictional subjects in Fitzgerald's works are entered in small capital letters.

Index

Index